T0384071

The ICT Malaise

The ICT Malaise

A Diagnosis and Cure for the
Dysfunctional Information and
Communication Technologies
Service-Delivery Workflow

Nadine Fruin

A PRODUCTIVITY PRESS BOOK

First edition published in 2019
by Routledge/Productivity Press
52 Vanderbilt Avenue, 11th Floor New York, NY 10017
2 Park Square, Milton Park, Abingdon, Oxon OX14 4RN, UK

© 2019 by Nadine Fruin
Routledge/Productivity Press is an imprint of Taylor & Francis Group, an Informa business

No claim to original U.S. Government works

Printed on acid-free paper

International Standard Book Number-13: 978-0-367-22856-9 (Hardback)

Library of Congress Cataloging-in-Publication Data

Names: Fruin, Nadine, author.
Title: The ICT malaise : a diagnosis and cure for the dysfunctional
information and communication technologies service-delivery workflow /
Nadine Fruin.
Description: New York, NY : Routledge, 2019. | Includes bibliographical
references and index.
Identifiers: LCCN 2019008127 (print) | LCCN 2019010501 (ebook) | ISBN
9780429277269 (e-Book) | ISBN 9780367228569 (hardback : alk. paper)
Subjects: LCSH: Information technology--Management.
Classification: LCC HD30.2 (ebook) | LCC HD30.2 .F78 2019 (print) | DDC
384.3/3068--dc23
LC record available at https://lccn.loc.gov/2019008127

Visit the Taylor & Francis Web site at
http://www.taylorandfrancis.com

To Uriel
With profound love and gratitude for being with me all the way
Thank You

To my parents
A heartfelt and loving thank you for teaching
me to have an independent mind

Aan Oma Dies

Lieve oma, dank voor de inspiratie. Voilà, zoals beloofd

In Memoriam

Lorenzo Cattani
13/1/1963 – 5/3/2019

Didn't I tell you?
I am an ocean, you are a fish;
do not go to the dry land,
it is me, who is your comforting body of water.

Rumi

Contents

Preface

Everything ICT-related is considered special, magical, full of promise and opportunity. With the help of ICT, we create a better world; we are more efficient, more productive and happier. The ICT infrastructure and environment are stable and flexible; there are few service disruptions and ICT projects are an example of skill, organization and great management, right? In reality, ICT is in an unedifying state, on all fronts.

It is quite clear that ICT has evolved from having a supporting part in businesses to occupying a major if not core role within any kind of organization, whether profit or non-profit. The rapidly succeeding technological developments and innovations with associated financial implications have led to outsourcing ICT functions to companies specialised in the provision of products and services: the service providers. The word service provider implies a service is provided to someone. It has a very positive ring to it. The customer receives the service and is satisfied. At least, considering the ad infinitum repeated mantra of customer satisfaction, we assume and presume they are satisfied. But it couldn't be less the case.

From ICT projects perpetually going past agreed delivery dates, being out of budget, out of scope and in general, out of touch with the customer, to the day-to-day routine operations mostly being about putting out big and small fires, service providers seem to have a talent for not delivering what they are supposedly experts at.

There are many examples of disastrously ill-managed ICT projects costing millions, governmental or commercial, spanning national borders and every single person working in ICT or being on the receiving end will have had at least one experience of a mega failure. There are also plenty of examples of nefarious service provider and customer interactions and not-so-constructive service provider and supplier relationships resulting in either a parting of ways, usually in a disagreeable manner, or a hardening of positions which results in additional customer dissatisfaction.

If the ICT department has internal customers, they tend to be viewed by the customer as expenditure; a black hole that swallows up funds and seldom delivers the quality service their colleagues expect and hope for. The external service provider is considered a necessary evil with a limitless appetite for trouble and an equally limitless appetite for money to solve the trouble they created themselves. Throw the various suppliers into the mix with their own agendas when supporting the service provider in its customer satisfying endeavour and we have a considerable technological and organizational complex reality to understand and manage.

The expansion of ICT presence in companies requires increasing need for structure and organization to enable these companies to manage the multiple phases of ICT service delivery: planning, design, development, build, test, support and maintenance.

In parallel with technological growth methods, methodologies and frameworks are developed to obtain and to keep a grip on the ever-increasing complexities ICT presents to the internal or external service provider, customer and supplier: how do we organise the customer facing functions? How do we organise the back office? How do we ensure quality? Keep costs under control? Manage the suppliers? Respect our agreement? How can we be efficient and effective? How do we make money? How do we ensure customer satisfaction?

Approaches to the management of the various phases of ICT product and service delivery were presented and formalised in the late eighties and early nineties of the past century, updated and new ones are continuously introduced. Professionals working in the ICT environment all know or have heard of ITIL, COBIT, Lean IT, Agile, Scrum, CMMI, DevOps, IT Governance and let us not forget the ISO standard, with its roots in 1947.

State of the art project management methodologies such as PMI/PMBOK, XP, Kanban, Waterfall, Prince 2, to name a few, are used world-wide to help companies manage their ICT projects, on time of course and within budget. Naturally the new optimized project management approach will be even better, faster and more effective and efficient.

Anything that is missed is handled with continuous improvement initiatives; in cycles, with 180 loops, 360 loops, with day boards, week boards and ultimately by The Board. We Plan, we Do, we Check and we Act furiously in our hamster wheel.

The focus tends to be heavily placed on implementing and improving processes. ITIL is a process-oriented approach to service management. Lean IT includes multiple dimensions needed to be focused on, processes a very emphasised one and COBIT 5, although having a very holistic approach, has also directed its attention primarily to processes. In fact, it is the most developed area with dedicated books. When implementing or optimizing this approach processes receive the most and frequently, the only attention. The idea is if we optimize processes, become more efficient and streamlined, we perform better, faster and the customer will be satisfied. In essence there is nothing wrong with this, because organising your workflows well is crucial for obtaining the performance you need to provide to the customer as a service provider or supplier.

Unfortunately, this focus hasn't achieved the result we had hoped. Notwithstanding all the optimizing, streamlining and becoming faster we still have problems, human beings a major one. Apart from the customers and suppliers, humans within the service provider organisation must be managed as well. Humans imply trouble. They are not bits and bytes, cannot just be clicked away. Let's be honest: the human part of ICT is not what technology focused people tend to be very good at or interested in.

With time we have come to realize that we cannot ignore the cumbersome human factor within ICT. We do have a customer after all, and uncomfortable customer surveys are published. ITIL introduced the "How to implement Service Management guide," with focus on how to overcome and manage resistance to the standardized process-oriented way of working and the importance of the cultural climate.

ITIL even includes specific roles for handling the relationship with and the satisfaction of the customer: the business relationship manager. COBIT 5 addresses the human aspect with the enablers: Culture, Ethics and Behaviour and People, Skills and Competencies. Lean IT places the Behaviour and Attitude dimension right at the core of the five dimensions crucial for an efficient and effective performing organisation.

This plethora of best practices, methodologies, methods and frameworks offer valuable guidelines, organizational tools and instruments to make sense out of the ICT service delivery landscape. But have me made sense out of it? Are we more in control now? Are the companies that have implemented, fine-tuned and optimized their ways of working, processes and IT-business alignment better off? *Are* they doing things better? Have we gained more understanding now that we have implemented numerous frameworks, one more holistic than the other?

We keep focusing on the same elements and forget or avoid—take your pick—to look a bit more closely if the approach we have adopted is really for our and the customer's benefit and if we really address the issues we must solve. And if we are focusing on the right things. Einstein's statement about what insanity is comes to mind: doing the same things over and over and expecting different results. We just do it faster now.

I don't think we are doing a good job. With 20 years of experience in the ICT sector in a variety of roles related to service management, process and project management and as a professional in management of organizational change, I think we are on the wrong track. I don't see more customer satisfaction, I don't see better service delivery. I don't see enough healthy constructive business relationships. Instead I see frustrated and unhappy customers, I see poor quality products and services, I see choices being made that are always solely money driven, never quality driven, and I see a lot of so-called leaders and managers opting out of honest and authentic leadership and management. I see a lot of money making.

The purpose of this book is to delve into how we got into the above-described situation and question the premises and assumptions about the goals we should be aiming for as service providers, customers and suppliers. It shines its light on the good, the bad and the ugly of ICT business practices. It addresses human (business) interactions and relations and how the above-mentioned parties treat their own employees and business partners with the ensuing desired and undesired consequences.

It is a critical reflection on the technology push of ICT and the quality of their delivery and support to the receiving parties and individuals. ICT companies don't produce products and provide services for fun or to add value; what drives them is to make money and add value to their own coffers. The message that they are doing it for the benefit of the customer is a nicely packaged marketing slogan. They even manage to make us customers believe we asked for it ourselves. Customers and users should understand this and keep a cool head when making important ICT related decisions. They are not just a passive party that has to accept every innovation and development as an undeniable reality and they needn't run at the same panting pace as the ICT companies.

This book's intention is to pause for a moment; instead of just racing full-speed down the path ICT companies are wanting us to go, let's rein in our horses and take a breath and then another, look behind us, assess where we are now and decide which road we want to take, how we want to do that and at what speed.

The structure of the book is as follows. Chapter 1 briefly traces the origin and development of ICT service provision, the challenges service providers face internally and externally and the ongoing disastrously executed ICT projects. It reminds us that the service provider's core business consists of facilitating and managing the information flow. The methodologies, best practice approaches, methods and frameworks created, and communication flows established to enable ICT delivery are put under the loop to define the situation we are in now, and how (un)happy all parties seemingly are with it.

Chapter 2 explains the causes of the current deplorable ICT service delivery reality and how we all breathlessly race along with innovation and money blinders on, but without enough critical questioning. It looks at the impact and effect of that chosen way of working on employees, partners, customers and suppliers. It deals with the human aspect of technology. Not with artificial intelligence or robots but with actual human beings.

Chapter 3 discusses fear. It dwells on the ethical and moral dilemmas ICT professionals face, the impact it has on them often resulting in stress, rise of sick leave, burn out, disillusionment, leaving the company or turning into a zombie, the walking corporate dead. The culture of fear is often consciously cultivated by management. It is something we should eliminate if we desire to have constructive and successful business interactions and outcomes.

Chapter 4 describes how we can do things differently. It gives guidelines on the necessary mental and organizational uncluttering. It is not enough to just put your house in order with optimized processes but some thorough mental spring-cleaning needs to be done. It is time to get rid of psychological waste. It invites us to take a hard look at ourselves, be aware of the corporate and business dynamics and make conscious well-informed decisions for the benefit of all: customers, service providers, suppliers and for all the people who work there. Of course, my suggestions can be ignored or absorbed and acted upon. Personally, I think we can and must do much better than we are doing now. The book ends with a short conclusion with some final thoughts and musings.

Users of ICT and ICT professionals, in the role of either service provider, supplier or customer are invited to put their feet up on their desks, lean back and do a little soul searching and reflection: on how they handle their affairs, if they feel good about them and about how they handle the most challenging affair of all: themselves.

Acknowledgments

Although writing itself is a solitary enterprise, everything that leads up to actually putting ideas on paper is done within a social context, with colleagues, professionals from all those companies I worked for and with; with students, friends, and family, as well as strangers who have crossed my path and with whom I have shared animated conversations that trigger a new thought process. I thank all those people, also the ones who are not here anymore or who are no longer in my life, but who endure in their writings, in verbal and nonverbal expressions, and in spirit.

I would like to give very special thanks to my mother who has endured the whole writing adventure up close and only the way mothers can: supportive, with admirable patience, and participating actively. She got into the groove of the book and provided me with interesting articles and useful ideas. Thank you for putting up with my endless monologues and for sharing the drama, as well as the fun.

Another heartfelt thank you is for JC. Your advice, not only in relation to the book, but to life in general, and your generosity to take the time to listen to me with such grace and understanding made all the difference and will stay with me forever. Thank you.

A big thank you goes to Dr. Plácido Moreno Felices, illustration wizard, both in design and in speed. My simple sketches were transformed into beautiful figures and you were able to translate my ideas into pictures. I am also grateful for your kind words during the writing process. Gracias.

Author

Nadine Fruin is an independent ICT consultant and trainer and works internationally as owner of Fruin Consultancy & Training, based in the Netherlands. She holds a Master degree in Organizational Change Management from the Vrije Universiteit of Amsterdam. She was Master Trainer Lean IT for ITpreneurs in 2016 and 2017, giving numerous sessions on behalf of the Lean IT Association in English and Spanish for professionals worldwide.

She is the creator of the Galileo Service Management Framework, developed in 2016–2017 for Spaceopal GmbH, which successfully secured the bid to be the Galileo Service Operator with the European GNSS Agency as customer. She is a consultant and trainer for Shipley Associates, a company with international presence which helps and enables companies worldwide with the preparation of complex bids with training, coaching or taking over parts of the tender preparation.

Over the past 20 years she has fulfilled a variety of roles such as process and service manager, trainer, coach, organizational change manager and business developer in multiple organizations worldwide, covering all types of private and public institutions on the service provider, supplier and customer side of business.

Endorsements

"A valuable, practical guide for navigating through ICT turbulence and dynamics. A lighthouse for the human side of ICT."

—Erik van de Loo
Director Executive Masters in Change,
INSEAD Professor of Organisational
Behaviour, INSEAD Business School

"The ICT Malaise is a different and thorough point of view on the dysfunctional approach the world has taken to information and technology. In an era of exponential changes where humans are rendered obsolete at the same pace of technology, it is fundamental to go back to basics on why we lead and innovate in the first place."

—Silvio Rugolo
VP, Global Sales, BMC Software,
Digital Service Operations

If future generations are to remember us more with gratitude than sorrow, we must achieve more than just the miracles of technology. We must also leave them a glimpse of the world as it was created, not just as it looked when we got through with it.

Lyndon B. Johnson

1

The Sorry State of Affairs

Information makes the world go around
Methodologies, models and frameworks galore
The ICT Bermuda Triangle: Service Providers, Customers and Suppliers

INFORMATION MAKES THE WORLD GO AROUND

The eighties and nineties were exciting times. For those involved in technology this was nothing new; they were aware something big was coming. The non-technology-minded individuals and companies were getting an inkling of intriguing new possibilities and were only just beginning to enter this new reality we find completely normal nowadays. We went from the introduction in the professional world of e-mail, word processing, files and folders, to internet and the digitization of information and communication. If you aren't digitized, if you're not on the web, you don't exist.

The introduction of ICT (Information and Communication Technology) into the professional environment and the ensuing enablement of faster and easier business interactions meant that this new aspect of business had to be managed and supported. Computer experts who understood this mysterious world of technology made things happen, solved problems and helped the often technology-ignorant user get back on track and online so that he could continue working. They were our colleagues, part of the new ICT department and reachable via the help desk, often situated right there on the work floor with us. ICT evolved, the customer business saw its advantages and potential benefits and so demand for IT products increased. The first years of ICT were an adventure, full of promise and the excitement of discovering a whole new world. Indeed, the World Wide Web.

Initially ICT departments were focused on technology, uptime and upgrades and they needed to react to cries of help from the users when there were problems. But customers needed more than having their problems solved; they needed ICT to answer their questions, understand their business issues, come up with solutions and anticipate needs. A reactive helpdesk wasn't enough anymore: the provision of services required a much broader and completer way of handling, managing and approaching ICT. Service providers, whether internal or external, came into being and their scope was the information flow, facilitated by technology.

This shift in focus meant going from a technology-oriented approach to an information flow one, from being primarily reactive to (trying to be) more proactive, not just providing support but delivering services, not aligning ICT to business, but integrating ICT with business. It is now considered a strategic asset. We have chief information officers (CIOs) who assist chief executives with defining and shaping strategy. ICT has become the business. It also means that the environment we must manage has gone from a relatively simple one initially to a very complex reality currently with multiple interdependencies, relationships and stakeholders. And let's not forget the promise of disruptive innovations that mesmerize us in no small measure and the potential of Big Data and Artificial Intelligence.

To understand the current situation service providers, customers and suppliers are in and the challenges they face considering the future and most importantly, if they are up to the task, we will have a look at how they have handled their affairs so far. The term lessons learned was coined as such for a reason.

In the rest of this chapter I will raise issues regarding the ICT service provider, supplier and customer relations, based on my 21 years of experience working in different capacities for all three mentioned parties and based on reports, surveys and papers on the subjects by other experts in their respective fields. I aim to identify problem areas and raise questions as food for thought. Certainly, there are service providers and suppliers who have their affairs in order and there will be customers who are satisfied with the service they receive. However, although there will be areas which function relatively well, there are always aspects which are overlooked, or which don't get (enough) attention. I focus on those areas, on the ones not functioning well or which are not addressed at all. These have unfortunate consequences and make our (business) lives more difficult than necessary. Overall, I consider there is still much work to be done; I focus on that work in this first chapter. In the following chapters I will zoom in on the causes of the dynamics I describe here and present ideas about the way forward.

From Reactive to Proactive and from Supporting to Delivering

The best practice approach to managing services, ITIL (Information Technology Infrastructure Library), uses the terms reactive and proactive when describing the activities of several of its defined processes. They make this distinction to clarify the differences e.g. when there are monitoring activities being performed as part of the Availability or Capacity Management processes and when these processes are in the phase of planning for the coming year, as described in the respective Availability and Capacity plans, being in these instances proactive. Problem Management usually starts out reactive, helping Incident management, and develops into a more proactive process, investigating trends in incidents and removing the errors that cause them, thus avoiding new ones from occurring.

These concepts can also be applied to understanding the development of ICT itself as a whole, particularly the position and role of ICT departments as internal service providers and later also to understand the outsourced functions to external service providers.

As described previously when ICT became part of the day-to-day business activities for professionals, the ICT department was primarily in a supporting role. The trigger for action was the customer needing help; the service provider focused on getting the service up and running again and respecting the response times as defined in SLAs (Service Level Agreements). The first and most needed activities and processes implemented for that purpose are the operation-oriented ones, such as incident, service request and access management and of course the service desk as first point of contact.

Additionally, all kinds of activities were going on in the background, unknown and unseen to the customer but necessary to ensure a stable ICT infrastructure. The customer didn't really care how they did it, as long as it worked and didn't cost too much. If a VIP called, the service desk would spring into action and not following the procedure was a minor detail.

However, only supporting the customer when asked for help wasn't enough considering the ever-increasing potential negative impact of non-well organized, planned and anticipated demand for ICT products and services. The service provider's proactive demeanor would permit a clear picture of the customer requirements, ICT projects delivered on time and within budget and generally, being in control. Proactive service provision leads to their infrastructure being sound and healthy and their pro-activeness results in satisfied customers. Or at least, that's the idea.

This transformation from helping to servicing, clearly expressed in the change of names from help desk to service desk, not only meant a different way for service providers to organize themselves but required a change in relating to the customer and specifically in the (IT) mindset.

Whereas principally the focus was on technology, now the situation demanded looking up from behind your screen and dealing with a person and anticipating his needs. You are required to not be solely happy because you solved an ICT riddle but because you satisfied a customer's need for help. You are required to put yourself in the customer's position and emphasize with them. And because of that you can respond to the demand of the customer.

Why do people work in ICT? Professionals are attracted to IT because they like it, they studied it because they find it fascinating and interesting and see possibilities. They like building something new and coming up with solutions. They like delving into its depths and shining their light on what they perceive as challenging issues. IT people are primarily technology oriented and adventurous obstacle takers. They are appreciated by non-technical oriented or interested beings because they help them out and solve their problems. When your car is broken down, the mechanic makes your day when he fixes it and you can drive into the sunset.

Customer orientation is perceived the most and in the most direct form when the customer needs help and contacts the service desk. The failure has already occurred, the work interruption is already there and a rescue operation is called for. The service provider scores points when he addresses the customer and the issue at hand in a decent, understanding way, is polite to the person on the other end of the line, mail or chat and when he solves the problem or answers the question. You could say, a reactive customer orientation, and when done well leads to customer satisfaction. Some statistics to bear in mind regarding customer orientation and satisfaction are provided by Help Scout, who published an e-book titled: *Customer Service: 75 Facts, Quotes & Statistics.*

The section titled "What Customers Think" quotes from *The Cost of Poor Customer Service* by Genesys Global Survey (2009) about what goes into a happy customer experience. Seventy-eight percent of customers say competent service representatives create that positive experience, and 38% of customers indicate it is personalization.

The following examples should also make service providers reconsider. *Customer Service Hell* by Brad Tuttle (2011) states "Eighty percent of companies say they deliver 'superior' customer service. Eight percent of people think these same companies deliver 'superior' customer service."

Based on the *Customer Experience Impact Report* by Harris Interactive/RightNow (2010) Help Scout summarizes that "In 2011, 86% of consumers quit doing business with a company because of a bad customer experience." And going back to the Genesys report, "By far, the MOST requested improvement from customers was Better Human Service. (40%) in comparison e.g. to 20% of Integrate More Channels and 15% Enriched Content and 15% Web Assistants or Avatars."

A good barometer for the degree of customer orientation in organizations and interest in customer satisfaction is how much attention is given to service desks. Since they are the ones with direct customer interaction, you can expect considerable attention is dedicated to service desks. Alas, they are still usually the last to be informed about anything (peak in incidents? Oh, probably the implementation of a change. Thanks for informing us.), never have time to be trained properly, are treated with disdain by second-line support and in general must figure it out pretty much all by themselves. Uh huh, the principal point of contact between customer and service provider, the service provider's business card so to speak, is so well equipped with skilled people and enough resources because we *truly* value customer satisfaction and orientation, don't we?

Customer orientation seems to mean giving an answer within the timeframe indicated by the SLA, but not necessarily giving the actual solution. Service desks are at the end of the line, to be invested in as little as possible; the high turnover tells the story. Customer orientation consists mostly in the business part of the relationship: selling a new product or service, hosting, the cloud, big data, digital transformation, etc. Quality support when the operation doesn't run smoothly tends not to be a priority as the above-mentioned examples showed. Another classic situation is to close incidents asap to comply with the SLA but without having solved the issue for the customer: aka creative incident registration administration; naturally these figures don't end up in statistical reports but are known by whomever works with SLAs.

If service providers are so customer focused, how come the number of incidents doesn't decrease considerably or more or less disappears? Incidents are symptoms of an ICT environment and infrastructure which are not healthy. They are the result of poorly designed and developed applications and systems being introduced into the live environment. The attitude seems to be to implement something as fast as possible into production. Après moi, le deluge. This approach is also visible when you look at how much importance is given to testing.

For example, to test a developed application is crucial to ensure customer satisfaction; you don't want to introduce errors, bugs and other unwanted elements into the live environment, the customer's environment, do you? Testing is part of all methodologies, best practices and frameworks, but it seems this period of making sure anything undesirable doesn't make its way into the live environment must be shortened as much as possible.

The attitude now is to go live, and correct and improve as we go along. The fact that the customer is confronted with regular and frequent downtime doesn't seem to be a major concern. Just a reminder: Within the Lean IT context, testing is a Necessary Value-Add, but more on that later.

A customer satisfaction practice nowadays is to ask the user to evaluate the service provided after every interaction. The user is asked to grade the service so that the service provider can use this information to improve the service delivered. It has become such a common and frequent practice it starts to annoy because you must dedicate additional time to something you are not interested in because you want to move on. You might want to leave a message or give feedback when things are bad, but usually you just want to get on with your business. Because of this, you fill out the form relatively fast. So how trustworthy are these surveys? Additionally, if you need to ask your customers continuously what they think of you, you seem rather out of touch with them in the first place. Do you need constant validation? Do you need your customer to tell you what is not working before you perceive it yourself? Or do you do these surveys to give the user the impression their opinion is important?

Responding to cries for help is reactive, but how proactive are service providers in their customer orientation? Pro-activeness is anticipating the customer's needs and acting on it, ensuring the workflows, products, services and communication flows are in place and active before the customer comes knocking on your door, even avoiding the customer needing to knock at all. Proactive customer orientation is about planning, designing and improving to ensure you have your house in order so your guests are at ease and taken care of. Are projects well planned and are the timelines respected? Is the result what the customer asked for? Are the projects within budget? Pro-activeness is having thought of issues in advance, making sure requirements are understood, penetrating an ICT issue to such a degree that you know which potential problems could be encountered and therefore anticipated. And you do all this because you are authentically customer oriented and customer satisfaction is important. If only… This helping out the less technology-versed customer by the knowledgeable has sadly evolved today to the know-it-alls, the ones who, in their own eyes, foresee the future and make customer business possible; more than that, without ICT the customer doesn't exist… and ICT knows it.

But today in the twenty-first century service providers and the people who work there are still mostly technology focused, apart from being business opportunity focused as well, and have not really, in their core, made that mindset shift to the necessary customer orientation. They think they have though. Because they repeat to the customer and to themselves they *are* customer oriented. I think they are trying to convince themselves as much as their customer. They are of the opinion they are doing quite a good job, they are avant-garde, shaping the world, something the customer just doesn't seem to get, all is hunky dory. We do what the customer wants, right? What are they complaining about? Ah, being a fly on the wall of ICT service providers when they speak about their customers…

We can deliberate about ICT service providers' reactive and proactive customer orientation, the presence, lack or sad state of it, and utter our opinion but how reactive and proactive is the customer's ICT orientation?

What about the customer? The customer still perceives ICT nowadays as it did in the old days. Just help me when I need you. Do it fast. And oh yes, you should be able to read my mind so that we both know what I *need* and *want*. If service providers aren't capable of these feats, we will not be satisfied. ICT still has a bad reputation and this stems from the past, from not delivering what I ask for, with the speed I want and with the price

I am willing to pay for it. ICT is the black hole where money disappeared into, whose ROI (return on investment) remains shady and which always involves problems.

A complaint often expressed by the service providers nowadays is the fact that the customer isn't capable or willing of communicating clearly what they want and need. Another complaint is that the customer is reluctant to share information about their business and future intentions which would enable service providers to get a better understanding of their customers' needs. Service providers still have the feeling they must pry the information out of the customer and do a lot of tugging to know what they should focus on and what is expected of them. And when they get the information, it is almost always tardy or very last minute forcing service providers into acrobatic contortions to deliver a product according to the timeline set by the customer, which of course hasn't moved along with the late information delivery and is still set on yesterday.

ICT, for customers, is not tangible and therefore hard to position and have a grip on. I can work, or I can't. Like electricity I flip the switch and there it is. I only notice when it isn't, and it bothers me when it isn't because I have things to do and have no time for this. And when I call the service desk I want them to solve my issue pronto because I have important business to tend to. And they treat me like an idiot because I don't get how ICT works so that pisses me off even more. The customer expects ICT to be pro-active, more or less read their minds without having to articulate clearly themselves what they want, and they still treat ICT as if they are in a mere supporting role. Additionally, ICT doesn't support its case very well because it sells itself—communication-wise—deplorably bad. They have fallen into the trap from the beginning, for example when they have their meetings with their customers to present the service reports as stated in the SLA, of highlighting service disruptions and faulty technology and not balancing it enough with all that does go well. For customers, ICT is a problem area and prone to cause headaches: whether due to bad service, non-transparent costs, not delivering on time, not delivering as required and always, always having excuses for it.

Within customer organizations it is normal to dedicate time and energy to Finance, Marketing and Sales; They must manage these areas if they want to be successful. The same should apply to ICT. You must manage ICT to such a degree and understand its ramifications to be able to interact accordingly with your service provider(s). Solely having demands and requirements and expecting to be serviced is not going to cut it, or at least, at the risk of slashing your own wrist. The role of the CIO is fundamental in the interaction with the service provider regarding this topic. How in control is the CIO and how serious is he taken by his own company and by service providers? Is outsourcing your core business—e.g. crucial information and communication flows—a good idea and is storing data in the cloud the best option? It is as if you have outsourced your blood vessels and blood streams to an outside body. Are customers aware enough of the risks?

A lot of customer organizations are still out of their depth. Most of them still don't have enough ICT knowledge to be able to truly assess ICT propositions and the next best thing service providers present them. Just as Finance, Sales or Marketing experts, customers need ICT experts. They need critical minded people who understand ICT and don't automatically think a priori all ICT innovations are marvelous and the solution to everything. And so, do they listen to their CIO? Is he regarded as a partner on the same level as the other C-suite executives? Is ICT perceived as a strategic asset or it regarded as a cost and not as an investment?

The way the relationship and role of customer and service provider has evolved is visible in *need* and *want*: the customer *wants* the innovation being hyped, the new big thing, the solution to everything. I am in, I am on top of my game, I am in control, riding the wave. A winner. Maybe they *need* something else. But service providers will sell them what they want because that is what they make money with and they will tell the customer that is what they need. It is as if a junkie asks his drug dealer if he needs another dose and expects an honest, concerned-for-his-wellbeing-answer.

The way things are now, service providers don't really need to consider adapting to the needs of customers and moving along with them; it is the other way around. The customers have to adapt to technology developments and are required to adapt to the ICT defined direction. Take it and swallow … or else choke.

When I describe the service provider way of being and doing it relates to their suppliers are well. They participate in the same merry-go-round which takes them into the ICT Bermuda triangle I describe later in this chapter.

From a Technology Focus to an Information Flow Focus

When I give training, be it ITIL, COBIT 5 (Control Objectives for Information and related Technology), or Lean IT, and my students are mostly from service providers, I always start out saying that their core business is information, not technology. Technology is the medium that enables information to travel and arrive. Service providers facilitate the creation, access, modification, storing and removal of information. COBIT stands for Control Objectives for Information and *related* Technology and defines this concept well. My students' reactions are always interesting. For some it is obvious, some are puzzled and others look pensive and seem to have never thought about information and technology in this way.

I highlight the difference between information and technology because it is crucial to understanding the role (and attitude) of the service provider and the expectations of the customer. The customer is primarily focused on information and the service provider tends to have his attention primarily on the technology. However, things are changing rapidly. Now several service providers have, apart from providing the technology to enable the flow of information, dedicated themselves not only to that information flow, but to the content itself and are focusing their business on that. More on this topic later.

As a customer I want to be able to access the information I need for my work (or pleasure) and be able to do with it what is needed within a certain timeframe. Of course, the PC has to boot, the programs I use should be up to date, bugless, not too slow, and I need to be online and capable of sending and receiving messages. The service providers see to it that the PC is working, the programs are up to date, debugged, not too slow and that the customer is connected. Of course, all according to the contract with the customer. When the service provider has taken care of all these aspects, information flows, is accessible and well-informed decisions can be made based on correct and complete information. When technology works, as a customer you can function, you can do your thing and don't think about it a lot. Only when there is no flow do we notice. And presently, when the flow goes where it shouldn't and the content of the information is (ab)used for propaganda, advertising, manipulation and spying.

The challenge and misbalance with service providers is the attention the technology aspects of service delivery receives versus the attention the information flow gets. And the awareness of the importance for the customer that information can flow. Service providers must see to it that the technology which enables the flow of data and information functions so that the information can travel well and without hiccups. It is not an either-or discussion: service providers must pay equal attention to the technology side of service delivery and support as to the data and information flow the technology facilitates. The attention, however, tends to go more to the technology side of their business—the part they like and understand—than to the fluid streams or flows of customer information, which involves customer orientation and interaction, not always a service provider's favorite activity, nor generally their biggest talent.

Information is not only important for our customers but of course also internally for the service providers organization itself. A service provider with lousy internal information flows won't be able to make those well informed business decisions and service his customers adequately. So how is the information flow within companies, whether they are service providers, customers or suppliers? And why is this important? It is important because it explains quite a few problems these three parties have internally and with each other. If we understand those dynamics we can avoid disappearing off radar into the Bermuda Triangle.

If, as a service provider, you can't manage your internal information flows well and as a consequence your communication flows, how can you have the pretension of doing it well for your customers? And how does the customer know what to ask for, what they need for their business, if their information flow stagnates and becomes muddy? Apart from the bad smell that is reaching us, we know that it can lead to major (business) environmental hazards.

The majority of organizations, irrespective of being more vertical or flat, consist of strategic, tactical and operational layers to manage their work. Information flows top-down from strategic, through tactical to operational level and flows bottom-up from operational via tactical to strategic level. Decisions are made on all levels based on the information available. Figure 1.1 depicts these information and communication flows.

When information is passed on from one layer to the other, a translation process takes place in the sense that the sender of the information will transmit the message in such a way that his audience understands it. Or said differently, the sender of the message adapts to the target group and will package and convey his message accordingly. This happens when a CEO on strategic level informs a middle manager on tactical level in a certain way, but the middle manager will present the information in such a manner to the work floor to ensure they understand it. At least, that is the idea.

We all played the game as children, and as adults, where you whisper a sentence into the ear of the person sitting next to you, who will whisper that same sentence to the person sitting next to him, etc., to discover, when the last person says the sentence out loud that it is completely different from the original one. The background, context and the way people's brain processes information varies enormously and is just as enormously underestimated

FIGURE 1.1
Healthy internal information and communication flows. Within organizations information and communication travel top-down from strategic level, through tactical to operational level via policies, meetings, emails, internal memoranda, phone, etc. These flows go bottom-up from operational level to tactical and to strategic level via reports, dashboards, meetings, etc., and as a result all three organizational levels are aligned.

when information is communicated top down. What language (wording) is being used, what tone of voice, is it clearly articulated or mumbled, how much time is used to convey the message? And what about the related body language? Within the ICT environment the pitfall is that communication is perceived as a 1 and 0 issue. This might work within the ICT service provider organization with people who are like minded but will create problems and misunderstandings when communicating with people who are not bit and byte oriented, such as the majority of customers.

On operational level we monitor and measure, produce reports on performance and send these to our bosses on tactical level. They will use the information to draft their own reports which go to strategic level. Based on these reports, and of course on other sources, well-informed decisions can be made for the benefit of the organization and its customers. If all goes well there is a healthy flow of information going bottom-up, as shown in Figure 1.1.

A healthy flow of information means the organization on all levels produces and receives the necessary information to function properly resulting in internal alignment. The internal alignment enables the organization to communicate in a consistent manner externally, for instance towards their customers and suppliers. Every layer, according to the nature of their activities and responsibility, interact on their level with their counterparts. Different kinds of information are shared with their

FIGURE 1.2
Customer satisfaction with consistent and aligned flows. A seamless flow of communication and information within a single organization will facilitate consistency and alignment on all three organizational levels between organizations and further customer satisfaction.

respective counterparts according to the organizational level they are active on. Figure 1.2 shows the described interactions.

All three layers have customer-facing people who have the responsibility to communicate adequately with their counterparts and so manage their customer relations. This implies they should be well aligned. In my experience, that is often not the case. Let's take ITIL and the processes with associated roles as an example, since ITIL is all about customers and the management of services for their benefit.

On strategic level a customer-facing role would be the BRM (Business Relationship Manager); on tactical level, the S(L)M (Service(Level) Manager); and on operational level, the Service Desk. Figure 1.3 shows where these roles are positioned. To transmit a consistent message according to the layer they are operating on, these three would have to be aware of issues on the various levels and inform each other on the performance, progress and status. How often do the BRM and S(L)M communicate with each other and what kind of information do they share? How often does the S(L)M have contact with the SD (Service Desk) or the head of the SD and what do they tell each other? They usually only have contact when reports e.g. are delivered by the SD to the S(L)M. Does the S(L)M report back to the SD and give them feedback about what was discussed with the customer? What about feedback from the BRM to the S(L)M? Do they confer or is there only contact when there is an escalation? And does the BRM ever talk to the SD? Is he interested in their input? Can the SD discuss issues with the BRM?

I haven't observed a lot of communication going on among these three layers apart from the obligatory periodic reports going bottom-up and mostly one way communication going top-down, either to inform about certain developments or to convey decisions or orders. I have noticed a lot

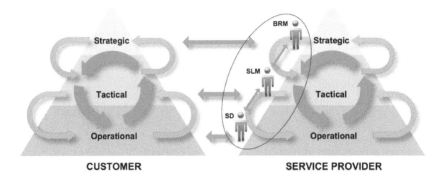

FIGURE 1.3
Efficient and effective internal relationships benefit the customer. Customer relationships improve when the customer facing roles and functions within the service provider organization communicate and share information with each other resulting in a consistent message being conveyed by all three organizational levels.

of miscommunication, incomplete sharing of information or simply non-alignment between the three layers, which expresses itself not only in internal frustration but also in clumsy interactions with the customer, on one, two or all three levels. This has a direct undesirable impact on customer satisfaction.

Another issue that creates plenty of problems is the respect or rather the disrespect of communication flows and acting according to your own and others' responsibility and accountability levels. Figure 1.4 shows

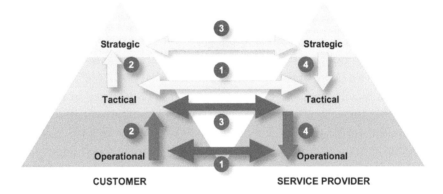

FIGURE 1.4
Constructive containment of escalations. Escalations from one organizational level to the other can serve as useful lessons learned and be reduced to minimal disruption for all involved when the respective levels handle the situation with responsibility, prudence and clear communication.

the communication flows in the case of escalations. They seem obvious but considering the amount of escalations taking place and the way the dynamic works in practice, no assumptions are made on the logic and I will go through the steps.

When a customer has a problem, he calls the service desk (number 1 on operational level). If he is unhappy with the treatment, if he feels he is not being listened to, if things go too slow in his opinion or if his call disappears into thin air, he might choose to escalate to a higher level within his company. Let's say from operational to tactical level (number 2).

His boss will contact the service provider, also on tactical level, for example the service level manager (number 3). The SLM will confer with the SD, ask what is going on, ask the SD to handle the issue in a certain way (number 4) and go back to his counterpart on the customer side to inform him. The customer will then inform the employee who escalated the issue. Lessons learned for all and hopefully there will not be a repetition of the matter. So far so good.

The same dynamic (numbers 1 to 4) exists for escalations from tactical to strategic level. Of course when you escalate something to strategic level, it should be serious. You don't escalate petty matters to a CIO or a CEO. They will also have contact with their counterparts on strategic level on the service provider side, who will talk to the service level manager on the tactical level. If necessary, the SLM will have contact with the SD or others on operational level depending on the issue. Lessons learned for all and hopefully there will not be a repetition of the matter. Again, so far so good.

The idea is that an issue is handled on the correct level and when escalated, managed at that level. Containment where it should be. If only things worked like this. We live in a perpetual escalation mode where professionals are being interrupted at a staggering rate to address matters that on lower levels cannot seem to be resolved. This goes for customers as well as service providers and suppliers.

What happens? As described before, when, for whatever reason, the customer is not satisfied with the received service, he escalates to tactical level (See Figure 1.5). Instead of handling it there, tactical level escalates to strategic level. When unnecessary issues are escalated the higher ups can get, to put it mildly, a bit pissed off. This dissatisfaction is transmitted to his counterpart on the service provider side, who also gets annoyed because he is confronted with a nuisance and so the degree of displeasure tends to go in crescendo as it is expressed to the lower layers, and of course the operational level getting most if not all of the blame. Since they can't

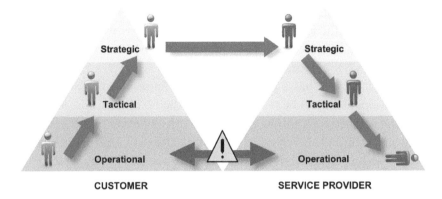

FIGURE 1.5
The perpetual escalation mode puts extra pressure on operations. The continuous escalations put unnecessary stress on professionals on operational level and can influence the organizational culture and customer relations negatively.

go any lower, they are stuck with it. Operations has to put up with quite an amount of disagreement, from the customer, supplier or internally from their own company.

Why are issues escalated so fast to the next layer and not managed on the appropriate level? Fear and because it is easier. Fear of taking responsibility when the s**t hits the fan and because it is easier to just let someone else do the hard work. We like the word manager linked to our name. It is not just a word; act like it. You are a manager in the good, the bad and the ugly. Your worth is shown when things are difficult. The problem can also be people don't have the mandate to make decisions and therefore escalate to higher ups. In essence, escalation is extremely inefficient. Apart from the time aspect, people are interrupted, meetings have to be scheduled, calls made and let's not underestimate the bad vibes and oooh yes, customer relations. And since this dynamic also exists within the organizations themselves, internal relationships won't benefit either.

When a matter is escalated the superior should first check if all has been done on the level where the issue originated. If not, hand it back to the person escalating, perhaps with some suggestions and advice how to manage it. It would be easy to think this only applies to the service provider somehow not doing his job. But the customer is, in my opinion, a champion in escalating and managing the question at hand as depicted in Figure 1.5. I am generalizing, but there is a strong notion among customers: I am the customer, I am King, therefore I am always right. This is also visible during ICT projects. The customer has this sense of (entitlement because he is paying) being able to change his mind at the last moment, wanting everything with a minimal price and needing it yesterday. Customers have a lack of discipline regarding ICT and expect ICT to solve it. It is as if I am sitting in a restaurant, have ordered a meal with all kinds of adjustments to the dish on the menu and after 20 minutes change my mind and want something altogether different. Or as if a house is being built according to the blueprint and during the building, when the wall is already in place, I want it somewhere else.

It is way too easy to merely blame ICT for everything that does not function the way it should in the eyes of the customer. Customers tend to want the maximum service for the minimum price. It doesn't work that way. So before signing the contract make sure you are getting what you want, need (!) and expect. And when you don't get what you want, it isn't a reason to throw a fit and escalate to your boss immediately.

Customers, however, do have reasons to be on the alert when wanting to conduct their business successfully. The service providers managing their information are managing their core business and if not their core business, all that enables their core business. Efficient, effective and protective information flow management is therefore crucial. A vital facet of this information flow are its privacy and security aspects. Therefore, let's store it all in the cloud. Safest place on earth. There are numerous articles on the advantages of cloud computing: efficiency, flexibility and cost reduction as there are plenty of articles on the dangers of storing data on the web: you are not in control of your data, cyber-attacks, lack of support, reliance on third parties and the risk of not being able to access your information, to name but a few. V3 published an article *Top 10 cloud computing risks and concerns* (2014) which states clearly the numerous risks. Apparently we have full confidence in the providers of this service. Of course they have excellent security measures in place, don't they? The bottom line is this: everything is hackable or penetrable, and it is easier now that it is out there. Considering the scandals going on right now with the big tech companies, maybe a bit of healthy mistrust is more adequate than singing hosanna with every new ICT development. And have we really weighed the cost and security aspects deeply enough? Quality service, meaning secure in this case, somehow always pays the price. Don't turn off your common sense, even if it costs more.

An additional factor we have to consider: the business of service providers is enabling information flow for their customers. The difference nowadays is they go or risk going from being the enablers of an unhindered flow to actually shifting their business to that which is flowing, their customer information, often without their knowledge. On top of that there are plenty tech companies exclusively dedicated to exploiting the information content their customers produce.

We are well aware of the crisis we are in now regarding the swirl of data and information exchanging hands for reasons that cannot withstand the light. Information certainly does make the world go round, but for whom? And at what price?

In the past we could count or counted on a basic decency of businesses (and governments) to safeguard our interests and wellbeing and respect privacy. That is long gone. Unfortunately, we cannot count on basic ethical behavior anymore. When you go into negotiations openly, you are considered naïve and out of touch with reality. When you talk about principles and ethics you are not taken seriously. You may hope the financial crisis taught us something but here we are, experiencing a global mistrust in the (ICT) institutions we once believed in and were proud of.

From Simple to Complex: Stability and Flexibility

Another reality our three actors (service provider, customer and supplier) were and are facing is the development of an initially relatively simple ICT environment that had to be managed to having to handle a complex environment with multiple players, relationships and interdependencies. This adds extra challenges to finding the right balance between stability of the ICT environment and it being sufficiently flexible to adapt to new situations. Maybe this is one of those rare occasions where ICT service providers and the customer want the same thing: stability. Not too many changes, not too many incidents, not too much drama. Change however is the only constant and whether we like it or not, we'll have to adjust to it.

The frameworks, models and methodologies, best practices and standards came and come into being precisely to create a certain logical order to get and keep a grip on the complexity, maintain stability, permit flexibility and last but not least, comply with legislation and contracts and ensure value creation for your customer. No mean feat. So have service providers responded to the challenge? Are customers satisfied?

Let's have a look at those elements that give us an indication on the above-mentioned challenges. We do it all for the customer and he pays after all so we will keep it simple. As a professional doing my work in a customer organization: can I boot my pc (or laptop) in the morning when I arrive, do I have an internet connection, can I access the information I need, is the connection fast enough? Or are there regular interruptions, do I have to call the service desk often, is the connection slow, are there uncomfortable crashes and freezes and bugs creating discomfort? Does my PC continuously need to be updated … with who knows what? On a grander scale: did we get what we paid for, has the project or new super app delivered according to the requirements, on time, on budget, is value created? Are there no security breaches, viruses, hacks, leaked or stolen information making its way to parties for shady purposes? To summarize, is the ICT environment stable (and secure) enough so that I can work efficiently and effectively as a user but does it have the flexibility that enables me, customer, to adapt efficiently and effectively to changes as well in order to remain competitive and add value to *my* customers?

I've answered these questions from a different perspective in the previous pages. Of course there are customers who are quite satisfied with their service provider because value is created, they are treated decently and they consider they are paying a just price. However, as we have seen before, the customer satisfaction numbers available are not overwhelming and I haven't met a customer yet who is content with the majority of these aspects: value creation, balance between price paid and service received, support given, personal treatment, transparent reporting, timely and adequate communication, security and privacy, pleasant relationships and no drama. Actually, the opposite is the case.

Service providers are appreciated and successful when they create value for their customers. To be more precise, it is their raison d'être. How is value creation achieved and what does it consist of? A clear depiction of the elements of value, as presented and used in the ITIL publications, is the breakdown into Utility and Warranty; I will quote from the ITIL Service Strategy guide (2011):

> Utility is the functionality offered by a product or service to meet a particular need. Utility can be summarized as 'what the service does', and can be used to determine whether a service is able to meet its required outcomes, or is 'fit for purpose'. The business value of an IT service is created by the combination of utility and warranty … Warranty (enough availability, capacity, continuity and security) is an essential part of design of a Service and should be built together with Utility. If this is not done, it may result in limited ability to deliver the Utility.

With Utility present, the service is Fit for Purpose; with all the elements of Warranty fulfilled, the service is Fit for Use. The combination of the two means value is created for the customer.

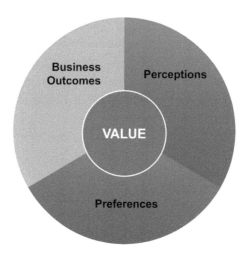

FIGURE 1.6
Value defined by objective and subjective elements. Effective service delivery and support is only possible if service providers as well as customers are aware that creating and receiving value depends on achieving the, objectively measured, desired business outcomes and on the subjective, and not so easily measured facets, of preferences and perceptions.

As shown in Figure 1.6 value is created when business outcomes are achieved, and vice versa, *but* value is also dependent on the perceptions and preferences the customer has of that value. And that's when the tricky part starts because where business outcomes based on utility and warranty are objective (in the sense they can be measured and calculated, metrics exist and KPIs-Key Performance Indicators—defined), perception and preferences are subjective, and often unconscious but they do define the person's behavior. Based on our upbringing, experiences and education human beings have ideas about how-things-should-work, what is better or worse, how we should communicate because it is valuable and that-is-how-it-should-be-done, apart from the measurable parts of a contract we have signed.

Customers sign a contract about the value to be created by the service provider, define KPIs and receive reports from the service providers who measure, manage, deliver and support the services to ensure the agreed upon utility and warranty are respected. Preferences and perceptions are managed as best as possible with appropriate communication and what we call expectation management. The value, the degree of excellence, of the service has the quality of what is agreed upon in the SLA.

Not only customers have preferences and perceptions. Within the service provider organization itself as well as for their suppliers, technicians have their preferences and perceptions about what a good ICT service should look like and how it should work and be used. Apart from the diverse ideas about value there is plenty of miscommunication *within* the service provider and their supplier organizations (on strategic, tactical and operational level) about quality and value. When you add to the equation the miscommunication *between* customer and service provider and service provider and supplier you have a windy sea to sail on. When the ICT environment was relatively simple it was manageable but now that we have multiple stakeholders involved and a complex ICT environment which is getting more so every day, stormy seas with high waves have to be navigated so as to avoid drowning.

It is not only the complexity which must be managed but the right balance between stability and flexibility has to be found as well. Obviously value is not created for the customer when the ICT environment is unstable, meaning the service is not available when the customer needs it, it is not secure enough or if it isn't continuous enough. Additionally, a customer wants and must adapt to changing realities so flexibility is paramount.

Ah, flexibility. What does flexibility mean? It is being pliant, tractable and is characterized by a ready capability to adapt to new, different, or changing requirements (Merriam-Webster). Flexibility means an organization is structured in such a way, that no matter what the (technological) developments are, the structure is so robust and well-functioning in the core, that it can bend with the winds without breaking. A service provider weathers storms and still attains its business outcomes because it is organized in such a manner that new services can be offered. Methodologies, best practices and standards help service providers be organized and flexible, on condition they are implemented correctly and people work accordingly. The whole reason companies implement COBIT, Lean, ITIL or a project management methodology, is no matter which new technological product or development is rearing its head, they are capable of absorbing, complying and continuing delivering and supporting services to their customer with the quality defined in the SLA. More on the methodology/best practice topic later in this chapter but suffice for now is understanding that flexibility is created, maintained and guaranteed within a service provider because the organization is well oiled with methodologies, best practices, clearly defined processes, etc. A well-oiled organization is flexible and as a consequence can react with agility.

Agility is important because technological developments come one after another and rapidly at that. The emphasis however nowadays seems to be on speed only. The word flexibility seems to have been translated into speed and is used as its synonym. It isn't. The capability of adjusting to changing requirements is obtained because you are well-oiled, not because you churn out more products by cutting corners on other aspects of the service, which normally means less quality, less robustness of the service, more bugs, more errors, questionable security, less ICT health overall. Cobbled together solutions, but cobbled up fast! It's not your fault! The *customer* asked for it, right? Haste makes waste comes to mind. Wasn't Lean about *eliminating* waste?

If I look at my 20 years of experience in the field, doing both consulting and training, sharing experiences with my colleagues and students, the same issues keep popping up: although there are best practices on designing and developing, testing and supporting, on the relationship between sales, development and operations, ICT service providers still manage to deliver products and services that are riddled with errors and customers are still negatively critical of them and not satisfied. The only difference is service providers do these things with more speed now, cordially helped by the increasing number of approaches focused on doing everything fast and faster.

The tunnel vision focus on speed has evolved into developing practices that enable the agility and although e.g. the Agile approach includes architecture and looks fine on paper, in practice the planning and designing phases seem to dwindle down to as short as possible timespans. Why do I highlight this? Because when a service goes live you notice how well it has been planned, designed, developed and tested. Operations is the sum of all those phases. Poor planning and/or poor designing and/or poor development and/or poor testing adds up to … surprise, surprise, poor live services. Ask the service desk about the peak in incidents and unavailability of the new service when a change has been implemented. The service desk is the thermometer of live services, incidents are the indicators and symptoms of their health. This is the reason the majority of organizations are so focused on the process incident management: aspirins have to be taken, compresses applied and emergency operations undertaken to keep the system up and running.

In the ICT world we speak a lot about continuous improvements. There are approaches and processes for identifying and implementing improvements. The Deming cycle, named after Dr. W. Edwards Deming,

FIGURE 1.7
Deming's continuous improvement cycle enhances gradual progress. The consistent and disciplined approach to improvements enables organizations to introduce new services and products, or to fine tune the existing ones making sure no steps are skipped and therefore safeguard the quality of the intended improvement.

is mostly at the basis of these approaches. Figure 1.7 depicts the Deming cycle used extensively in organizations today.

The Deming cycle emphasizes that before doing anything, you must Plan. Then you Do it, Check that you Do according to the Plan and if not Act upon it. Acting upon however, means Planning it first and then Doing it. And so on. When we look at how a project or new application or any other improvement initiative comes into being, for clarity, we can add design to the Plan phase as well as the preparation before going live with it. When we do go live eventually, there are no major upheavals because we had adequate planning, designing, testing and preparation of the transition before offering it to the customer for use. Figure 1.8 shows the addition of Design within the Plan phase. We could also add Testing there.

By the way, The Deming cycle depicted here is not correct, as Deming himself has indicated numerous times. He referred to it as

FIGURE 1.8
Solid Design before building. Within the Plan phase of the Deming cycle a thorough and thought through design is necessary before building or developing commences. This is to avoid backtracking and error correction once implemented which creates extra costs, in money and in reputation.

the Shewhart cycle: Plan, Do, **Study**, Act, the PDSA cycle. I will go into detail on this topic in Chapter 4.

So, if we follow the Deming cycle and we plan, design, build and test adequately before we go live, there shouldn't be major problems when the service actually goes live. The project was planned well so the service provider respected the deadline, worked within the budget and delivered the product the customer asked for. And value was created for the customer. Immediately the millions of euros or dollars come to mind which have gone and to this day still go down the drain in big projects due to lack of planning, poor design, changing requirements, insufficient oversight, inefficient work practices, clumsy communication, etc. Why? Because doing things well and with enough thoroughness is perceived as time consuming and boring. There are plenty of instances in the news as well (calling back cars due to faulty design for example) and we all know that fixing an error costs more than doing it right the first time round. Wasn't everything supposed to be smart now? That is the whole clue of Lean but it implies an attitude and behavior change which managers are often not willing to make. I will address the cause of this issue in detail in the next chapter.

So we are fine with delivering second rate and/or faulty products and services to the customer and the customer is left hanging. Imagine building a house without planning it, with no architect involved, without a design. Let's just start building and have our oops-moments along the way. We'll pour in some more money and keep going. We might end up with not enough sockets, walls where we didn't want them, too small windows, a leaky roof and brittle walls. We have a structure that resembles a house, is called a house but it won't be a home. So much for having created value.

When we do have architects, and an architecture, do we listen, do we develop based on the architecture? Do we take their input seriously? Do we test our products to make sure they work, do we check if we create value? Or do we do it la-la-la because there is no time … and it's not our fault because the *customer* wants it yesterday? Service providers as well as customers and suppliers are good at the blame game, and continue doing so even if they are veering off course into the Bermuda Triangle. It is what we call playing ping-pong: the ball gets hit onto the other's side as fast as possible to deal with the issue. Service providers, customers and suppliers seem to like ping pong a lot.

Considering the dependency all businesses have on ICT, it is unacceptable that such faulty structures can be built. There are frameworks, best practices and processes, e.g. TOGAF (The Open Group Architecture

Framework), that are dedicated to ensuring sane and healthy ICT services and products are constructed but if organizations don't work accordingly and cut corners continuously for the sole sake of speed, ergo money, we shouldn't be surprised if the roof collapses. Work smarter (creating value for your customer), not faster.

If we look at the Axelos survey of 2017 and at the processes implemented, the attention goes mostly to the firefighting operational processes, not to the ones necessary for a robust design, starting with a solid acquiring and understanding the customer requirements. We are stuck in the continuous loop of running around patching things, instead of introducing effective structural improvements. Are we authentically interested in improving or are we *saying* we are implementing improvements; are we using, e.g. the Lean approach or Continual Service Improvement best practices as a handy way out to manage all the errors we are introducing consciously into the live environment because we don't plan, design and test well? A different kind of throwing over the wall, cloaked in a recognized process and therefore accepted. Or do we invent yet again a new approach, DevOps (Development and Operations), to cover this issue? And is it effective?

The higher the complexity, interdependencies and potential disastrous impacts, the more the need for a clear picture, overview and grip on your business processes, which includes ICT related processes since you depend so heavily on them as a customer. For ICT service providers a clear picture, overview and grip are crucial, because that *is* your business. If service providers and suppliers don't have a grip now, if they don't deliver sound products and services based on a robust ICT infrastructure now, are they going to be in control in the (near) future if we look at the pace of developments? And are customers in control? Or do they merely swallow the technological hot cakes with gusto?

The new talk of the town is digital disruption. If we believe what is being published and said about its effects, the more reason to have your house in order, as a customer and as an ICT service provider. The eagerness with how digital disruption is approached, the fascination with the disruptiveness itself shows a craving for the dis-balance. Smooth operations are boring, a bit of peace is sad so let's create something that creates a jolt and say it is good, it's what everybody wants. It is like junkies craving the next kick. We don't want harmony, we want excitement, the oohhhs and the aahhhs. We'll worry when we have come down from our high.

From Business—IT Alignment and Business—IT Integration to Business—IT Mutation

When ICT began having an increasing presence in business performance the importance of being in sync with the customer business processes and understanding what the customer needed led to what was coined as Business-I(C)T Alignment. ICT had to be aligned with the customer on all levels: strategic, tactical and operational. Specific roles were identified on the ICT side to deal with the customer to make sure the demands and needs of the customer were understood and that a correct assessment could me made ICT wise on the feasibility, design and execution aspects.

In reality, the emphasis in the beginning was on the operational part of ICT; how do we execute what the customer asked for? The customer asked, ICT did it. That was the alignment. Before the existence of a CIO, it was primarily the CFO who had IT under his wing and who was accountable on C-level for the correct handling of ICT affairs, certainly in terms of money matters.

You can state that ICT was in the reactive mode. Leading in the relationship was the business, either as an internal or external customer, who would indicate what was required and ICT would see to it that those requirements were fulfilled. This relationship meant ICT was still primarily technology focused and had, overall, limited business comprehension. The limited business comprehension had to evolve rapidly into a more profound one, however, considering the speed of (ICT) developments and increasing benefits for the customers.

ICT became such an important part for and of the business that a mere alignment wasn't enough; ICT had to integrate the business (or the business had to integrate ICT, depends on how you see it) into its strategic, tactical and operational activities. ICT is integrated into business decisions because ICT can make business possible and have a positive effect in creating value for the customer.

The changing position of ICT is reflected in the changing role of the CIO. It has shifted from someone mostly concerned with the ICT infrastructure to someone who is required to not only understand technology but the effects technology has on the business and how ICT developments can create value for the customers, as well as for the ICT service provider itself of course. From a reactive to a proactive/anticipating capacity. This implies a CIO must be well versed in ICT and in business; quite a challenging role.

So how have the CIOs fared with the alignment and integration? Up till now the role of the CIO has varied: albeit the title, there were and still are CIOs who are IT managers and still focused primarily on technology, infrastructure, how to siphon IT to the cloud and how to save money. Others are performing more in alignment with their title, dedicated to information and the related technology that enables the flow and use of it. And I should add its security, considered very important in word and in print but where with high regularity the biggest breaches and muck ups happen, just follow the news.

An example is the EU General Data Protection Regulation (GDPR). Companies scrambling at the last moment to comply with the deadline. They knew this was coming since April 2016 but left it till the last instance to comply by May 2018. What does that tell you about the importance given to security and privacy issues? Protection of EU citizens from privacy and data breaches didn't seem to be the highest priority but more the financial penalties for non-compliance were the worry. Companies were changing the terms of use at the very last moment (May 2018!) to supposedly comply ... in print; but in deeds, in attitude? And what about the countries where there is no or minimal legislation and compliance regulation? That's the wild, wild west for you. How does a CIO fit into that context?

Was ICT ever aligned with the business? Ever integrated? Taking into account the moaning, perpetual escalations and overall dissatisfaction on customer, service provider and supplier side I would say there is still plenty to be done. We introduce and invent new methodologies and frameworks to address these issues but in reality there *are* plenty of frameworks that define and specify what has to be done; we just have to *do* it instead of introducing the new, hot holistic approach which supposedly is THE answer to our (short-term?) woes.

Again ITIL comes to mind, or COBIT 5. The five ITIL lifecycles are as clear as can be on the interaction between the customer and service provider, on alignment, on integration on all three organizational levels. The processes that are described cover the entire service lifecycle, from strategy to operations and how to implement improvements in any of these lifecycle stages.

It is very clear on the customer and service provider relationship, has dedicated roles, such as BRM (Business Relationship Manager), SLM (Service Level Manager) and explains the close necessary relationship between development teams and operations.

COBIT 5 is a Governance and Management framework which shows in a simple and clear way how stakeholder needs, influenced by multiple factors such as environment and technology developments, cascades down to enterprise goals, subsequently to IT-related goals and finally to goals which enable those IT goals, such as processes, organizational structures, people skills and competencies to name a few of the seven in total. This cascade enables you perfectly well to align or integrate, take your pick, business with ICT *if* you make the effort to do so. You can follow the flow and the logic top-down and bottom-up. An added value is the detail of e.g. the guide on the enabler Processes. No need to reinvent the wheel.

Now we have DevOps. DevOps has a strong focus on the cultural aspects and is tightly intertwined with Agile and Lean IT. Let us hope that all the beneficial aspects of DevOps, such as collaboration, eliminating waste and continuous integration and delivery get equal attention as time to market and that it isn't reduced in practice to mere speedy delivery by cutting corners of the other aspects. When that happens there will be something new after DevOps. To go even faster. There is nothing wrong with these new methodologies per se, but we will do what we have done so far: adapt it in such a way that the uncomfortable stuff such as quality, solid testing, documentation, etc., is ignored or sidelined. We leapfrog ahead. The fact we need to continuously improve after the application has gone live and need to solve a never ending flow of incidents indicates the before mentioned "stuff" which requires thoroughness in thinking and doing does not get the attention it should, notwithstanding the frameworks, methodologies and best practices which cover these issues.

Where do we stand now? I think we are going a step further than mere integration of ICT into the business. ICT is defining the business. It is becoming the driving force of business decisions, it is taking over. ICT is changing the DNA of companies, defining how organizations evolve and where the emphasis is put; in other words, we are talking about **Business-ICT mutation**.

ICT is becoming the business or has such a major impact on the business that it is actually changing the identity (and core values?) of the business. You cannot see it as two different elements anymore: Business is ICT and ICT is business. Of course, the question is what the business is mutating into? In biology there are types of mutation and depending on the type it has small consequences or potential big (bad) ones. When you get changes to the genes, the DNA is modified. We get mutants. What are businesses mutating into? What are the consequences? Do we care? As long as we make a lot of money, have our big house, big car and fast boat and we can brag about it on social media, we don't seem to mind very much.

What does mutation mean for business-ICT relationships? Is ICT going to define what we do, what the options are? Is the (ICT) system leading, or are we?

A potential mutagen is what is described as Artificial Intelligence (AI) The disruptive developments such as self-learning machines are hailed as being able to provide us with many benefits, e.g. in healthcare and fraud detection. What are they learning? What are we teaching? Are we going to outsource decision making to machines, to algorithms? What will their decisions be based on? The benefit of the customer, the benefit of the ser-vice provider or of the supplier? And which benefit? And how do we define benefit? In terms of money, quality, efficiency, effectiveness, the common good or just mine?

I wonder what kind of mutation will take place with self-learning machines. Are we trying to outsource human-being-ness to machines so that it saves us from the effort of taking responsibility for our actions and the impact those have on others? If you are not a self-learning machine, if you're not in the system, it can't be done; if you're not in the system, you don't exist. If machines "learn" to be human, humans (must) "learn" to be machines with chips inserted into their bodies? What are *we* mutating into? The corporate walking dead?

Servicing the customer can be taken over by machines, and supposedly this would make it better and faster. But if machines are learning from humans and their data, and currently the ICT-business relationship is not something to be overly enthusiastic about and still needs a lot of work to improve it, we would be fooling ourselves that all will be better with these new tools. A fool with a tool is still a fool. We would just make the foolishness more efficient and effective.

The present and future is information. It is about pools of data, connect-ing and linking them and using the results. Organizations are licking their lips with the possibilities of having so much access and control over data and information flows and what can be done with them. IoT (Internet of Things), AI and machine learning makes the access and control not only faster, it makes the scope ever broader.

As a customer, as an end user, as a civilian I can't trust companies (or governmental institutions) anymore to take care of me, protect my data and information from being accessed, taken and (ab)used. My information has become an item to be sold and exploited. We have become (disposable) products of corporate companies and states.

The CIO's role considering the present and future developments will be a very important one, and it is up to every one of them to define what they stand for and whose interests they represent. We must have more emphasis on the strategic and tactical aspects of ICT service delivery as a service provider and on strategic and tactical aspects regarding the use of ICT as a customer. Adopting every new ICT development that is being hyped by ICT companies is not a strategy, it is opening your mouth obediently on command to be spoon fed the new IT hot cake.

A C-suite level CIO is needed on all sides: the customer, the service provider and the supplier. Someone who has overview and who understands the impact and consequences of developments on business, on people, on society and who is able to convey a balanced and well informed message to his colleagues on C-level. But a CIO with a real added value does not exempt CEOs, CFOs and all other C-executives of understanding IT and taking an active interest in it: don't depend on a CIO too much.

Get versed on information yourself and the impact the use and management of data and information have on your company and on your customers. That's not something you merely delegate to someone else.

Innovation is very much in the picture. There is a lot of talk about its importance and all the potential added value for multiple areas of (business) life. What has always caught my attention is that innovation is solely related to technological innovations: self-driving cars, drones, rockets to Mars, smart fridges and smart homes. For those working in ICT and technology the concepts of Technology, Processes and People are common to denote these three elements are necessary to focus on to ensure success with a balanced approach. In many organizations innovation in processes seems to consist in introducing new processes or new approaches to provide services and/or products better and faster. As we have seen in the previous pages, the focus is strongly on going faster, but not (qualitatively) better or smarter in my opinion. Innovation in the area of people is given the least importance. Every once in a while employees go to courses or trainings to obtain foremostly a certificate, not necessarily more knowledge. Creating an environment that fosters positive relationships, productive creativity and ethical professionalism is relegated to a company's spare time.

The Capability Maturity Model® for Business Development written by Paul Deighton and Howard Nutt (Version 2.02, November 2016) gives a very comprehensive overview of the five best practice maturity levels for business development (Level 1: Initial, Level 2: Managed, Level 3: Defined, Level 4: Quantitatively Managed, Level 5: Optimizing) and when innovation and transformation is viable and actually achieved. Innovation is only possible when all the dimensions have reached a certain maturity level, in this case level 4. There are very few companies who manage to reach a maturity level 4, or even desire to do so. What is so interesting about this model, about CMM in general, are the identified growth paths such as Customer, Leadership, People, Process Management and Support. Per mentioned capability category the five maturity levels are detailed and explained, and People are included. Instead of continuous innovations and introducing new processes, new tools, new IT, new people (?) we should put our house in order and actually *use* and *work* according to the processes we have in place, optimize them and focus perhaps a bit more on quality instead of speed. Disruptive technological and IT innovations sound thrilling; so does that go hand in hand with disruptive processes as well as disruptive people?

The incredible achievements which can be obtained with AI and innovative developments are fascinating. Goethe's "The Sorcerer's Apprentice" is a reminder that not all magical possibilities are innocent looking; respectful and conscious awareness and application would be wise. We are enchanted with Artificial Intelligence and the self-learning capabilities of machines and all the benefits we can reap from these. What about enhancing real intelligence, the human one. Do we? How do *we* learn? *Do* we develop? Is there space for *us* to self-learn, self-develop and enhance self-awareness. Do organizations facilitate our human self-learning?

METHODOLOGIES, MODELS AND FRAMEWORKS GALORE

In medieval times Mappae Mundi were used to illustrate the principles of, among other things, the Earth's sphericity and climate zones and the concepts of cardinal directions, distant lands, history and mythology. The mappae mundi, both from their concept and in their concrete practice, are founded on a systematically geometric projection of the known world. The basis of this projection, however, is not geographical surveying but the harmonious order of God's creation. (Brigitte Englisch (2002) *Ordo orbis terrae: Die Weltsicht in den Mappae mundi des frühen und hohen Mittelalters, Berlin.*)

Frameworks, methodologies and models can be seen in the same light. We try to map and visualize our reality in a structured and harmonious order which enables us to come to grips with the complexity of our organizational creations. The more complex our reality, the more we need to understand all the elements we must manage and control.

So here we are in the twenty-first century: ever increasing complexity in content and scope and increasing at a formidable speed. Having our house in order is paramount. The available frameworks, methodologies, models, best practices and standards abound, so the question arises which to choose, *if* we have to choose, which can be combined, where they overlap, what to do about that, which addresses exactly what, if they work; in short, how do we approach these approaches to order?

Before we enter the world of specific ICT frameworks, let's give a moment's thought to the current situation of the existing methodologies, models, etc., in our companies. Most organizations already have quite a few present and add new ones regularly. Which needs do these new ones answer? Are the existing ones, which are updated and improved continuously as well, not working? *Are* they being improved continuously? Are the methodologies not working, the processes not well defined, the information flow not addressed, not managed? Are issues not registered, not shared with the relevant parties, not documented? Is that a problem of the approach, method or standard itself or is it that people are not *working* according to the methodology or framework?

Have all the relevant processes been implemented? Do people know their responsibilities and act upon them? Do they document, do they follow the procedure, do they act? Do they *understand* the framework? Do they know what *the point is* of the methodology? Has anyone ever *explained* it? Or was it assumed they knew? What happens: when it isn't understood, well, the framework is not working, it doesn't cover our needs so what we'll do is implement that new methodology everyone is talking about at the moment to solve the problem. We often introduce new approaches, etc., due to lack of understanding, lack of taking time to penetrate the core intention of the existing one, lack of patience and lack of willingness to just think and do the hard work.

Focusing on ICT, there are plenty of frameworks, etc., to help us order our (digitally based) organizational creations. New ones are constantly being promoted so it is easy not see the wood for the trees if you don't understand them clearly. Let's have a look at what we are dealing with. The following paragraphs mention a variety of frameworks, best practices, methodologies, etc. There are many more, focusing on specific areas, so although the list is not complete (there are too many to name here) the ones mentioned are the ones most commonly used in the management of services environment.

Management of Information

Service providers and suppliers deliver and support services and products and use service management frameworks and methodologies with all kinds of variations to the original theme, being ITIL. You could state that companies take ITIL as a basis, pour their organizational sauce over it and name it e.g. MOF (Microsoft Operations Framework), eTom (Enhanced Telecom Operations Map. In 2013 changed to mean: Business Process Framework) or the ACME Service Management Framework. In the end, they address the same issues and tailor it to their specific organizational reality or industry. Within the service management context, VeriSM™ (Service Management Approach for the digital age) is a new model with focus on the service management environment with its service culture and structure.

COBIT 5 is also directed at the management of information and related technology but adds the Governance dimension and is more extensive and complete than ITIL. COBIT doesn't just focus on processes, but identifies multiple enablers, seven to be exact, which are needed to achieve enterprise goals and respond to stakeholder needs: Principles, policies and frameworks, Processes, Organizational structures, Culture, ethics and behavior, Information, Services, infrastructure and applications and People, skills and competences.

The Balanced Scorecard and related IT Balanced Scorecard are worth mentioning. The balanced scorecard is the basis of COBIT 5 and the cascade top down from Governance to the enablers on operational level.

Lean management and Lean IT focus on maximizing customer value while minimizing waste. It comes down to creating more value for the customer with only those resources needed for the value creation. The focus points are how to improve service quality, customer satisfaction and therefore create real value to the business. It consists of five dimensions, interestingly with Behavior and Attitude at the core and the other dimensions Customer, Performance, Organization and Process. Six Sigma is often mentioned in combination with Lean, since the approach to identifying and introducing improvements after discovering defects is what Six Sigma is about. It is based on statistical information and the DMAIC methodology. (Define, Measure, Analyze, Improve and Control).

Let's not forget the basic structure and organization of it all: architecture, described in The Open Group Architecture Framework (TOGAF).

Of course we have the quality standards poured into ISO norms, highlighting either service management, quality, security, etc. Formal audits are possible and provide (re-) assurance to customers.

Management of Projects

We use the structure of a project to get work done that has a clear beginning and an end; it has a predefined end-result as a deliverable. Once the product has been built, it is handed over to the existing organization and the project is dissolved. All project management methodologies are focused on how to get from the beginning to the end, on time, on budget and delivering the end result the customer asked for and agreed on.

So take your pick which project management approach you want to use: PRINCE2 (Projects IN Controlled Environments), PMP (Project Management Professional), PMBOK (Project Management Body Of Knowledge) and when we speak of a portfolio of projects, we have Program management methodologies such as MSP (Managing Successful Programmes) and MoP (Management of Portfolios).

Management of Software Development

Nowadays specific approaches with emphasis on the efficient and effective development of applications such as the framework RUP (Rational Unified Process) and its variations, Agile Scrum, XP (Extreme Programming), DevOps, either approached as a project or not, are used.

To manage risks we have M_O_R (Management of Risk) and certainly we mustn't forget the best practice CMMI, with its origins in software development and identifying the 5 capability maturity levels of processes and which has applied this approach to a model on managing the Supply chain (CMMI-ACQ), product and service development (CMMI-DEV), managing and delivering services (CMMI-SVC) and People CMM. CMM is also the basis for a Capability Maturity Model for Business Development.

Management of Security and Privacy

The management of cybersecurity and cyber resilience are in the fore and will obtain more and more relevance and prevalence as we continue digitizing everything. There is the ISO standard ISO27001 and new standards, frameworks and associated certifications are becoming more known such as NIST cybersecurity, CISA (Certified Information Systems Auditor), CISM (Certified Information Systems Manager) or Resilia, to name just a few.

With all the above mentioned frameworks, models, best practices and standards and the list certainly isn't complete, we can expect, and so can the customer, the management of information, projects, software development and security to function well. To summarize, we have our affairs in order and are therefore capable of providing an orderly service provision and support. That will be the day.

Does top management have a clear vision and strategy which are translated down to consistent tactical and operational plans? Are the things we do on operational level tied into the tactical goals and do those support the strategic goals? Do we understand, on any level *why* we do things, for which purpose and how our activities add value to the customer outcomes? Does top management have the overview and are they capable of explaining to the other organizational levels what it is we are actually trying to achieve? Can we all say: ah yes, I see the coherence and consistency. I see the logic, I get the picture. But I often wonder: *Is* there a picture?

In the previous pages and as seen in Figures 1.1 to 1.3, I discussed the necessity of having an internal order first, a degree of organizational maturity and process capability with corresponding information and communication flows to be able to relate to the customer and deliver and support IT services and products adequately. That is the reason for using frameworks, etc., because it helps us with the (overall) picture, on various abstraction levels, to have a grip on our IT complexity. Choosing which best practices, models and approaches to use to achieve this grip is fundamental.

My intention is not to promote any particular framework or model; it is up to organizations to decide which one they need, works for them, which they like and feel comfortable with. I will however highlight issues which I think are not functioning well and I will use the approaches commonly present in service providers, suppliers and customer organizations to make my point and question their use and effectiveness. Figure 1.9 gives an overview of some of the frameworks and methodologies and best practices mentioned.

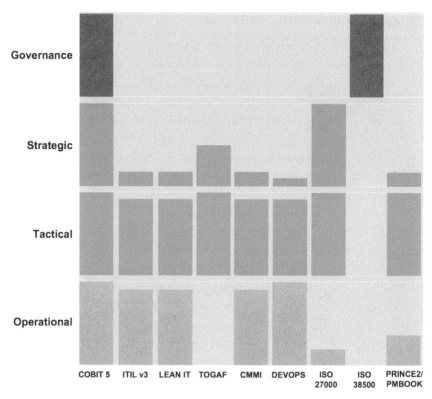

FIGURE 1.9
A selection of frameworks, methodologies and best practices. An overview of frameworks, etc., and which organizational level they cover can help make the wisest choice for the needs of your organization and help avoid excessive overlap.

What all the frameworks, methodologies, etc., have in common, independently from them being focused on the management of services, projects, information, software development, etc., is that there is a structured approach, a logic, which is subdivided into steps or phases. Following a certain sequence, having identified stages helps to ensure that no crucial elements are missed and that the end result we have in mind and on paper (as agreed) will be obtained. Achieving (the closest state to) perfection is not possible by haphazard jumping about but with a consistent and perseverant step-by-step logic and determination. If you want to make harmonious music or play the piano well you'll have to practice in a certain way, with discipline and focus. If you want to enjoy a beautiful garden in summer, you'll have to tend to it, weed, water and trim it for the plants to blossom. Or, to get into the spiritual mood, acquiring illumination is the result of following the path and keeping to it, taking one step at a time. There are no quick and easy fixes to Walhalla.

Let's have a look at Lean IT. When I teach or talk about Lean I always show or invite people to have a look at videos of Toyota and how they manufacture their automobiles. Their Toyota Production System is what we know today as Lean manufacturing and applied to ICT as Lean IT. When you look at those videos, it is clear they are in control, they are organized and there is no mucking about in their focus on delivering a manufactured car for the just in time delivery required by the customer.

The Lean terminology indicates clearly where the focus lies: voice of the customer, customer value, value streams, non-value-add activities and waste. Achieving that customer value by seeking perfection, focusing on pull by the customer and not push by the service provider and identifying the value stream and its flow.

Another important part of Lean to understand well are the five dimensions that have to be addressed if you want to add value to your customer with no wasteful activities. The five dimensions are: behavior and attitude, performance, customer, process and organization. The dimension behavior and attitude is always depicted positioned in the middle. The focus of Lean IT is strongly on this aspect. Logically so, since the success of the other dimensions derive from the "right" attitude and behavior: you are always on the alert about what you can improve, what you can make better. In other words, Lean is a mindset focused on value creation, perfection and improving.

Lean IT doesn't tell you how a process or value stream should be structured but it gives you guidelines on how to optimize your processes and how to eliminate waste. In short, lean IT is an excellent addition to any approach or best practice that focuses on how to organize your processes. You could call Lean IT the missing link to all those process oriented methodologies because it highlights the aspect all those other approaches do not pay attention to: the people factor, with its core in attitude and behavior, which expresses itself in the culture of an organization. The culture of an organization defines the way it does business and in the end, makes or breaks it.

You would expect then that the Lean way of working is much sought after; alas, the survey of Gartner 2017 shows it is not implemented a lot. Surprise? No, because working the Lean way implies having the courage to take a long and hard look at your own attitude and behavior and what kind of attitude and behavior you are encouraging within your company. It can be quite confrontational. There is quite a difference between the traditional management mindset and Lean mindset, such as: management has all the answers versus managers asking the right questions, managers do the thinking, employees should stick to doing, managers know best, decide and a certain amount of defects are unavoidable versus management which facilitates their employees to add value and defects can and should be eliminated, to name a few. Ah, this is perhaps an uncomfortable truth for plenty a manager with a certain self-image. To be avoided at all costs!

And so we do not eliminate waste, listen to the voice of the customer, try to achieve flow of our value streams and take a facilitating role in regards to our employees. Do we walk about, listen, show respect and ask our employees why they do things a certain way to truly get to the core of an issue? Are we authentically interested?

How does ITIL fit into this picture? ITIL as best practice with its five lifecycle stages—service strategy, design, transition, operation and continual service improvement—states which processes are important per lifecycle and describes their flow. It has evolved with new ICT developments from its original form of the 1980s till the latest version 3 of 2011. Version 4 is being developed and will be introduced in Q1 of 2019. They have adopted the speed aspect and disruptiveness by eliminating the whole service lifecycle.

ITIL version 3 is a clear and coherent approach and identifies the necessary activities and processes to be able to deliver and support services to customers according to the SLA. Also here you would expect companies adopting this approach to have satisfied customers and services and products being delivered and supported just in time, according to customer needs and quality wishes. This is not the case unfortunately. Why not? Because service providers cherry pick which processes they implement and therefore lose the logical coherence the combination of the lifecycles offer.

Additionally, they dedicate their attention the most to the operational processes and to the Change Management process because the interest is in being able to implement new or modified services and products asap. The Strategy and fore mostly the Design lifecycle phase with its processes are the least (well) implemented. Why? Because a decent design requires a certain amount of time and resources which companies nor customers are willing to dedicate to these activities. It is all about doing, not too much about thinking before you act. A solid design requires a resource investment which seems not to be part of our business model anymore. With minimal resources, the maximum must be achieved. That implies the maximum can't be at a very high level anymore. Quality has gone down because we simply don't dedicate the resources and time to do something well.

Apart from the fact we simply just don't have the interest anymore to do something right the first time, to take pride in designing a well thought-through product or service, to deliver value that will last. We've become sloppy in our thinking, in our designing, in our testing, sloppy in our communication, in our efforts and sloppy in our service delivery and support.

The whole point of the service lifecycle phases and related processes is to help service organizations manage their service delivery and support so that they can add value to their customers and to work in an effective and efficient way while adding that value. Do we seriously make the effort to understand our customers' desires or do we make assumptions? How well is Business Relationship Management working? And Demand management? Are these processes defined and implemented? Are these activities consciously performed? Portfolio management sounds nice, but do we actually have an overview and manage our services, whether they are in a planning phase, are being developed or are already active? Do we know how the processes relate to each other, what their dependencies and interdependencies are?

We know the importance of Availability and Capacity management. Do we have these processes with related responsibilities in place? Do we design for these for a new service? Do we consider the service continuity aspects when designing, include vendor issues and last but not least pay enough attention to security? Do we have these processes in place which ensure the critical elements are covered in a disciplined and complete way or do we manage them a bit comme ci, comme ça? What about Service Level Management? Is there a relationship with your counterpart on the customer side or does this role consist mainly of producing reports on KPIs (Key Performance Indicators) and that's it? We know processes are transversal and their great value consists in stating clearly what has to be done to enable service provision. So when implementing processes and involving the relevant parties silos shouldn't be an issue or at least, should not be defining the end result. If only.

And the Change management process? Defined to permit control and overview of all changes implemented into the live environment to ensure the least negative impact on that environment, for the benefit of the customer. It has become a sham. If there is a certain safeguarding going on, it is experienced as a show stopper. Speed is the name of the game, damn the consequences. Of course if the designs and development were decent and the testing done adequately, the quality of the products being implemented would be such that you don't end up in a continuous fixing-the-lousiness-loop aka continuous service improvement.

What I see in practice is still a lot of silo thinking and acting, no clearly defined processes, no clearly defined responsibilities (RACI: Responsibility, Accountability, Consulted, Informed), partial implementations and not enough follow through. A new so called quick fix framework or methodology is not the answer; just be disciplined, implement and work with the ones you have. Stop being slaves to hypes. Develop a consistent service delivery and support vision, an overview or framework that positions you as a company and use and stick to a logical approach.

As managers, are you in control and on top of your game, are you shaping and enabling a constructive work environment and work practices that achieve the end results you can be proud of and comfortable with? Or do you outsource that responsibility to the new approach, the magical methodology?

Will Agile and DevOps solve your issues? Do they help you work more efficiently and more effectively and deliver added value to the customer? I find it incomprehensible that ICT companies, after all those years, still can't seem to get a grip on customer requirements. Or are they irrelevant? They are the basis of product and service development and there are numerous best practices, methodologies, etc., around that clarify the steps to be taken to understand and acquire them but we manage to take a side road all too often. Just look at the amount of disastrous projects. Not a new approach or methodology is needed, but ICT must shape up and mature. If interested, CMM(I) (Capability Maturity Model Integration) can help you assess where you stand on the maturity ladder.

We mustn't forget that ICT hasn't been around for a very long time. ICT is like the new kid in town, the young man who is enthusiastic and ready to conquer the world. There isn't a lot of patience for the existing structures and best practices from other industries. We are different, we are going to change the world so all the "old" is to be done away with because they are not necessary anymore and are impeding development. Fine, but are you charging ahead with tech-blinders on or is there a logic and structured approach to ensure the provision of added value for your customer?

COBIT 5 helps organizations come to grips with the governance and management of enterprise IT. COBIT 5 is a very complete and in their own words, holistic, framework. It covers all the organizational levels and relevant principles such as: meeting stakeholder needs, covering the enterprise end to end, applying a single integrated framework, enabling a holistic approach and separating governance from management. The cascade depicting the clear translation from stakeholder needs down to enterprise goals, IT related goals and to its lowest, most detailed level, the concrete enabler goals makes it extremely practical and useful.

The guides on the enablers Processes and Information are very detailed. The same goes for the professional guides, such as Implementation. If ICT organizations or departments have doubts about how and what to implement and what potential root causes and success factors exist in relation to particular challenges they are facing the mentioned books will cater very well to your needs. But again, this is no quick fix but a sound integrated approach and framework that requires discipline and vision to make it work. And the question remains when the other enabler guides such as Principles, policies and frameworks, Organizational structures and Culture, ethics and behavior will finally be published. It seems we tend to get stuck in the processes and forget about the other aspects which are so crucial to healthy customer, service provider and supplier interactions.

The ICT reality we are dealing with is not an integrated one. The solid, thought-through and logical best practices and approaches are either implemented partially, not well or hardly at all. Do managers on strategic level have a vision and focus, are they able to translate those into tactical and operational plans and activities, do they have perseverance and staying power or are they victims of the new fad, the new hype and go into reactive overdrive?

The strategy (of a customer) seems to be to implement any new wow! approach flung into the ether by technology companies (service providers/ suppliers). The service providers and suppliers' strategy seem to be to drive and advertise every new ICT development, irrespective of a real customer need for it. The Lean principles regarding pull seem to evaporate into thin air with the merciless push by interested parties and willing and passive ears on the service provider as well as the customer side to invite them in. Is the new motto: disruptive developments require disruptive solutions and disruptive methodologies? Let's pop a pill and get our momentous high?

Do new ICT developments and new services imply new methodologies, new models, etc.? New is not bad at all, but what about the existing ones? Do we improve them, fine tune them? We introduce new approaches continuously to supposedly address important issues but often they are a mere rehash of the old put into a new jacket with hip new terminology and they continue avoiding the real issues: quality service provision, a positive communication and information flow, clearly defined activities, for example described in processes, clearly defined links and dependencies and clarity for all people involved what their responsibilities are so that they act accordingly.

To conclude the topic on best practices, methodologies, standards, frameworks, etc., we can state that they have all come into being to make things work better, more efficient and more effective. They can be powerful, positive and useful. *If* we work accordingly, *if* we don't eliminate the elements we don't like. *If* we use them in a larger context within the organization, *if* we don't cut corners such as we do with designing and testing.

They can help service providers, suppliers and customers achieve the needed stability and flexibility. Flexibility, as we saw, is being pliant, tractable and is characterized by a ready capability to adapt to new, different, or changing requirements. The methodologies, frameworks, models, etc., with their related processes and workflows enhance the capability to adapt. They ensure *quick* adaptation but also *qualitative* adaptation. They are the oil in the machine.

They help organizations to structure complex subject matter, get an overview of a reality with multiple actors and dependencies and interdependencies, to be in control, know how to approach an intricate matter and how to proceed. They clarify the actors involved (RACI: Responsible, Accountable, Consulted, Informed) and define decision-making dynamics. With this internal organizational order a service provider will be able to respond to the changing needs and external developments of their customers. (CMM; first internal order, this enables in level 4 and 5 to really respond to changing environments and new developments.) Internal order leads to external order. A consistent and coherent pace is necessary, not jumping from one thing to the other. We need a bit of staying power; not leapfrog tactics.

The vision and focus of strategic management defines and directs the internal and external order. They have the coherent a consistent master vision because they have oversight and perception (ideally) of internal and external dynamics. Their vision is a sort of overall framework of all the frameworks. Does it exist? Do they have it? Organizational harmony and flow can only be created when there is a conductor, a gardener, a master chef who have that overview and order. In the organizational context, this means a group, team, multiple people on the various management levels must have this overview.

Look at nature as an example: a tree needs time to grow, to take root. So does a plant before it can flower. When we buy fruit which has been plucked green and underdeveloped, we notice that in the taste. Not enough time on the tree, not enough sunshine. Instead of waiting for the mango to grow into a juicy and tasteful beautiful fruit, we accept less quality, less pleasure and less health.

Food needs time for preparation. A cake needs a certain time in the oven to rise. We don't half bake it. So why would we implement or develop half-baked ideas, products or services? What we do is sit in front of the oven peering in, willing the chocolate cake to bake faster. In ICT we do force it to go faster, and there we are, with half-baked products and services being implemented and offered to the customer. And who peers? The service provider AND the customer, both impatient; one because he wants the money asap and the other because he wants a bite NOW. And so they take the cake out of the oven before its time. They keep each other in a nice twist that way. Maybe we should stuff ourselves a bit less with under baked (hyped up) products and enjoy just a few, but more savory and wholesome meals.

Sound best practices and approaches are being skipped because we want easy digestible bites which gives us instant satisfaction. So we invent new, easily consumable methodologies in bite-sized pieces that require the least effort on the service provider's as well as the customer's side: ICT fast food.

Discipline, consistency, awareness: a (chef) cook needs all those qualities to serve us a wonderful meal we are willing to pay for as customers. So executives on strategic level: what are you cooking?

THE ICT BERMUDA TRIANGLE: SERVICE PROVIDERS, CUSTOMERS AND SUPPLIERS

In the previous pages we have looked at the development of ICT, the ICT service provider's relationship with its customers and suppliers, how that relationship evolved, the aspects which influence(d) the relationship and where we stand now. For clarification I will give a summary of the issues discussed. I will use the Technology, Process and People triangle (Figure 1.10) often used in the ICT service management world to indicate the three aspects which need to be addressed and managed internally, meaning within the service provider, within the customer organization and within

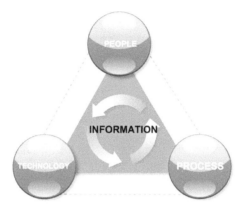

FIGURE 1.10
Process, People and Technology focus enables success. Information and communication will flow better when all the three dimensions important in achieving business outcomes are equally taken into consideration.

the supplier organization. These aspects influence and define the interaction and way of doing business externally, between the three parties, e.g. how the service provider delivers and supports services and products to and for the customer and how the customer interacts with the service provider.

The following pages sum up the issues discussed in this chapter grouped per the mentioned Process, People and Technology dimension. I have placed the items under the dimension where the most weight of the matter lies; obviously there are interfaces and overlap between the aspects, such as People-Process issues, People-Technology points of interest and Process-Technology elements.

As indicated, this triangle represents the issues present internally within all three parties: service provider, customer and supplier. Subsequently I will name the most important issues *between* the three parties, the dynamic and topics which are not going well and need, in my opinion, more attention, as a result of the "misbalanced" process, people and technology aspects. There will be some overlap as well since they are not isolated areas. Once again, it is a summary of the points discussed in this chapter and not complete for more issues will appear in the subsequent chapters as we delve deeper. It reads as the traffic light system used for projects to indicate the progress or in this case, the status: red, orange or green. The green status light, however, is absent from the summaries below; you will have to make do with the red and orange only.

Process

- Process, communication and information flows are not clearly defined and documented.
- Although there are processes, workstreams or value chains in place they are often not adhered to and corners are cut resulting in a haphazard, reactive way of working, aka running around like headless chickens.
- The manner in which processes are implemented doesn't facilitate flexibility and stability. This is caused by lack of awareness of the important issues, lack of knowledge, interest or/and patience. Or the combination of all of them.
- There is a serious lack of decent Design to get it right the first time. The same goes for Testing. Testing is considered a nuisance and a show stopper.
- There is little or no interest in doing things well structurally. Fire fighting is preferred to ensuring errors are avoided or eliminated in advance (before going live).
- We adopt (new) frameworks, best practices, methodologies, etc., without enough (fore)thought about if and how they serve our organizational purposes; Additionally, there is a lack of staying power to implement, e.g. all the necessary processes, and implement them well, meaning thoroughly, with attention to detail.
- Continual improvement: in spirit or in name only? Are structural improvements made and root causes eliminated or do we just apply patches to correct poor planning, designing and developing?
- Ethical considerations and implications are not or insufficently addressed.
- The main focus is still on technology instead of on information flows. And when they are addressed, there is a misbalance in the attention they get with the resulting undesired consequences.

People

- Service Provider/Supplier mindset:
  - Helping and servicing
  - Reactive and proactive
  - Technology focus and Information focus

Instead of a balance of all the above mentioned aspects, there is a misbalance with a preference for reactive, helping, technology focus. Wait till the customer shouts and then do something.

- *Service provider's customer orientation:* Are service providers authentically customer oriented and is that reflected in the SLA? Customer orientation should be visible in words and deeds but these (can) divert considerably.
- *Customer satisfaction:* A much used mantra. Service providers use this term a lot but they are trying to convince themselves more it seems than actually providing it.
- The influence and awareness of perceptions, preferences, attitude and behaviour of yourself, of the service provider, of the customer and of the supplier is not present enough or not understood at all.
- *Customer mindset:* need and want. The customer doesn't make the distinction between need and want, doesn't understand it or doesn't want to understand it, although they need to.
- *Customer's ICT orientation:* The customer is still too much out of its depth in regards to understanding ICT (at least the basics). The knowledge and/or understanding is either absent or marginally present. The responsibility to get a grip on ICT is outsourced to the CIO by the other C-level executives so they don't have to make a real effort themselves.
- *Executives and management:* (within all three parties)
  - *Strategic level:* not enough attention to proper communication to tactical and operational level. Not enough checking the message has been received.
    - Ever increasing pressure on employees to deliver more with less. Something is going to give and does.
- *Management overview and control lacking:* The service provider, customer and supplier houses are not in order and the ICT reality is becoming more complex, dependent and interdependent by the day.
  - *C-suite executives:* the role of CIO varies considerably. It can be very strategic or still quite operational. This can lead to confusion. Additionally, the position of the CIO in regards to the other C-level executives is not always clear.
    - Morals and ethics in relation to ICT decision making should be more under the spotlight. It doesn't get enough attention, usually only when the organization ends up in the news.
- More (thorough) thinking first is needed, then the doing/executing. We rush into doing because then we think we are making progress. We talk about the Deming cycle, but we don't act accordingly.

- Many oops moments due to flight forward, instead of robust thinking, planning, designing, testing and execution.
- *Quality mindset:* attention and concern for quality has been phased out. It is considered to be too much of a hassle. It is easier to fine-tune as we go along, when it is in production and the customer notices.
- People don't follow the process that has been defined to achieve a concrete result because it is not well defined, not explained well or there is a lack of professional discipline.
- The approaches, best practices, frameworks and methodologies are not (well) understood and are only partially implemented.
- Frameworks, methodologies, best practices, etc., focus primarily on the process aspect and not enough on people's roles within the process: RACI
- Organizations want quick and easy solutions and are not willing to do the basic ground work.
- There is a lack of staying power and management is easily distracted by new hyped up approaches.
- Organizations are in a perpetual escalation mode: due to lack of clarity, fear of responsibility or just plain laziness. This distracts people from the actual work, impacts the environment negatively and is a highly inefficient way to use the already limited resources.
- Fewer human resources and more work leads to mistakes, cutting corners and not delivering the quality they should.
- Operational level is duped and forced to fire fighting. The Service Desk, the company's business card and first (and often only) point of contact, doesn't get the resources to do their job well and are frequently treated appallingly by their own company. Operations have to save the day and the backs of people who are often the ones causing the problems.
- Process, information and communication flows are not clearly defined by those responsible and not explained and/or enforced when not followed.
- Do we consider our people the most important if not crucial resource of the company? Do we treat them that way? Do we enable their growth so the company will grow?
- Are professionals mutating into the walking corporate dead? And (smart) machines into better manageable human AI resources?
- Moral and ethical uncomfortable topics? Ah, let's not reflect too much.

Technology

- Increase in complexity, interdependency and dependency but decrease in control, overview and order.
- Adoption of new technologies without enough forethought whether they serve our organizational purpose.
- Lack of an architecture. This means a lack of oversight and control which puts healthy and safe growth at risk.
- The main focus is still on technology instead of on information flows or if there is attention for information, it is often misbalanced.
- Unhealthy interest in the information itself which the customers produce: shift to management of informational content rather than to the adequate flow of the information.
- Lack of sufficient security and privacy measures. Due to lack of interest?
- *Stability and flexibility:* flexibility has translated into speed and stability has been phased out it seems and been translated into craving constant disruption.
- *Focus on speed:* rapid developing in detritus of value (creation). The new motto is: more, more, more, faster, faster, faster: ICT fast food to gorge on.
- *Professionals:* quantitative and qualitative issues: do we have *enough* SMEs (Subject Matter Experts) Do we *have* people with the necessary subject matter expertise? Do we train them (on time)?

The ICT Bermuda Triangle: Service Providers, Customers and Suppliers

The red and orange traffic light status of the Process, People and Technology mentioned points influence and impact the interactions *between* service providers, customers and suppliers and are summarized in the following pages. This has led to a drain of energy, good intentions, of positive actions and constructive communications into a bottomless dark pit, as visualized in Figure 1.11. Welcome to the ICT Bermuda Triangle.

1. *Disconnect organizational levels:* The information and communication flows top down from strategic to tactical and operational level are not clearly defined, understood in content and/or in importance.

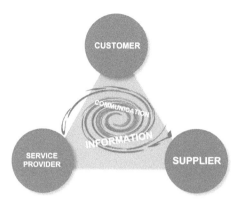

FIGURE 1.11
The Bermuda Triangle dynamic in ICT. The relationships between service providers, customers and suppliers can veer off course when the information and communication flows. stagnate or become murky resulting in customer dissatisfaction, ineffective and inefficient service delivery and support, mounting costs and damaged reputations.

The same applies to the flows bottom-up, e.g. in reports produced and used. These stagnating flows have unwanted repercussions because decisions are based on them. Communication and the manner in which we do this is often underestimated or assumed to be obvious and clear. The internal communication and information flow difficulties influence, impact and become visible in the quality and (un)pleasantness of interactions with customers and suppliers. The roles and responsibilities on the various levels and specifically the customer facing ones, are crucial for constructive interactions, as shown in Figures 1.1 through 1.3.

2. *Over-escalation:* The issues summarized in the previous point lead to a tendency to escalate rapidly to the next level. One of the causes for swift escalation are the unclear communication and information flows and grey-area responsibilities; another cause is *fear* of taking responsibility and finding it easier for someone else to face up to difficult or uneasy situations and do the hard work. The continuous escalating is very inefficient because it keeps people on all levels from doing their normal day to day work and directing their energy to constructive topics. Constant firefighting and interruption for—frequently—petty issues is draining. Figures 1.4 and 1.5 show the escalation dynamic.

   Blaming others for the uncomfortable situations creates an unpleasant and unconstructive environment, within the organization itself as well as between organizations. What is our own contribution to the situation at hand?

3. *Service provision quality decline:* Service providers say their focus is on value creation for the customer. Is that so? We can address the fact that value creation depends on utility and warranty and that both are needed but do service providers practice what they preach and are they organized in such a way they are capable of value creation through utility and warranty? A major warranty issue is security and privacy. This is clearly lacking with severe consequences for customers. Value depends on the desired business outcomes and most importantly on the customer preferences and perceptions. Figure 1.6 depicts this topic. However, service providers and suppliers have their own desired business outcomes, preferences and perceptions and these influence and define, consciously and unconsciously, their ideas and deeds in relation to value creation. Indeed, how conscious *are* all three parties of their preferences and perceptions regarding value creation?

   A customer perceives value when the ICT infrastructure and service delivery and support is stable and flexible. Flexibility, however, has become a synonym for speed. Fast development, fast production and fast implementation invites cutting corners on solid design, testing and implementation, leading to poor quality. Deteriorating thinking, doing and as a result deteriorating quality of products and services. Figures 1.7 and 1.8 show this based on the Deming cycle.

   Value creation and quality concerns have shifted from the customer to the ICT service providers and suppliers. The way things are now, service providers don't really need to consider adapting to the needs of customers and moving along with them; it has become the other way around. The customers have to adapt to technology developments and are required to go along with the ICT defined direction, and pronto, please!

4. *Disastrous projects*: Organizations, either profit or non-profit, initiating and managing ICT projects have a talent or predilection to mess them up: in time, money and/or quality. Within budget, respecting timelines and delivering according to specifications continues being an unsurmountable challenge for many ICT projects. Project leaders and managers used to have, and still have in many cases, the star reputation of working on the next big important thing. They have a special status and are considered the company heroes. Some more

heroism in simply complying as agreed would be nice for a change. Especially now, when we get excited about the relished disruptive innovations. Considering the track record of failed ICT projects and the amount of money disappearing into the Bermuda Triangle a bit of prudence might not be a bad idea.

Customers play an important role as well in the non-compliance. How pro-active are they, how ICT oriented are they and how much do they collaborate to ensure the project is a success? ICT can't just whip a bunny out of the hat when you ask for it.

5. *Customer (dis)satisfaction:* All of the above mentioned topics cause customer dissatisfaction. If customers, service providers and suppliers don't have their internal affairs in order, this is noticeable in the interactions with outside parties.

We mustn't forget ICT hasn't been around for that long and that the developments go at an extremely accelerated pace. This young industry wants to mature at an ever increasing speed, but the foundations need to be solid and robust to ensure healthy growth. This tends to be forgotten or waved away as irrelevant. The risk taking has increased and we can ask ourselves if there is enough awareness and serious consideration of the consequences of the high speed of developments and introduction of the so called new best ICT thing. Risk management involves risk analysis and then the countermeasures which can be taken to manage the identified risks. Have we analyzed enough, are the risks identified and do we have countermeasures in place?

ICT organizations have maneuvered themselves into a position of not being able to say no to the customer. The customer asked or demanded and ICT delivered. Miscommunication between the parties meant this misbalanced relationship got worse over time. ICT companies don't say no anymore when they cannot deliver or when it is impossible what the customer asks, but because they never want to say no to a business possibility.

Additionally, ICT companies, service providers, suppliers and big tech have had an advantage over customers because they had knowledge the customers didn't have, and didn't understand, especially the impact and repercussions of digitizing their data and information. This has led them to considering themselves as special, and of occupying a so called select position. This has also fed their arrogance. Arrogance in the treatment of the ignorant customer, arrogance in service delivery and support, in the quality of services and products offered and arrogance in the communication.

Plenty of customers think they know all about ICT when they have understood only a little. They have gotten used to demanding, snapping fingers and being catered to. Many do not take enough own responsibility to deliver the necessary information on time and fully to the service provider. Although they do not have their own information and communication flows in place they expect ICT to solve it with technology, by waving its magic wand and with their own minimal input. How much responsibility do customers have for their own dissatisfaction?

6. *Costs headache:* How does the customer perceive money needed for ICT? Is it a cost or is it an investment? Is there clarity on the ROI? Are the customers' expectations realistic? These questions can apply to any industry but considering the pace and impact of developments, the considerable dependency and risks and the potential business opportunities ICT provides, the money aspect of ICT is a crucial factor to manage, and to manage well. We have seen, however, that ICT projects are not overwhelmingly well managed money wise; we all know toe curling cases which defy common sense. If ICT is so important for organizations, there is no excuse for mismanagement of private or public money and letting millions go down the drain because there wasn't decent planning, oversight or communication. Frequently, ICT service providers, to obtain deals, offer prices for services that are not aligned with the customer expectation and are not realistic. There is enormous competition, so they offer something they know they cannot or will not deliver. Nice low prices are wonderful, but know as a customer what you can expect quality wise and be realistic with expectations. A lot of frustration, anger and escalation could be avoided.

We focus purely on money when we mention costs. What about the cost to security, privacy, independence or reputation when we become enthusiastic about the newest gadget, latest development, awesome disruption and faster everything? Are we willing to pay the price for the ICT fast food offered?

7. *Overload of frameworks, methodologies, best practices etc.:* They abound and are useful. They help us structure, organize and manage workflows, technology and people. They show the connections and interfaces with other parties. They clarify roles and responsibilities.

They provide overview of the complex reality which must be controlled and managed. The question is which are relevant for your company, which to choose, which can be combined, which complement each other, how much time is needed for implementation, for maintenance, etc. Figure 1.9 gives an overview of some of the frameworks, methodologies and best practices used.

The speed with which ICT fast food is practically pushed down our throats has sped up the development of frameworks, methodologies, etc., as well. More and faster is better seems to be the battle cry. When a framework, best practice or methodology has been developed on robust foundations and when it is implemented just as seriously, a constant new adoption of the old in a new jacket is not necessary. Applying common sense, fine tuning what you have and taking the time to think it through, penetrating the chosen framework deep enough and adhering to it means you do not need to be hyped up about every next best thing. The methodologies, frameworks, etc., enhance the capability to adapt to a changing environment. They enable quick adaptation but are certainly there for qualitative adjustment as well, to enable the flow: they are the oil in the machine.

8. *Not in control:* Albeit the multiple frameworks, methodologies, best practices, etc. ICT service providers are not more in control, neither are suppliers nor customers. On the contrary, looking at the pervasive dissatisfaction, the scandals, hacks and accumulating malpractices coming to the surface, we are less in control.

Not only CIOs are in a difficult position, but the other C-suite executives must realize they are responsible and accountable for the decisions made which define the trajectory of the organization, including the ICT decisions which shape business interactions, within their own companies, and externally, with other parties. Do you have an overview, do you have a vision? Are you aware of the risks?

ICT and business have never been aligned or integrated. And now our much more complex reality is embracing ICT-business mutation: the digitization of everything and everyone. So, sorcerer's apprentice, are you, are we, in control?

9. *Security and privacy nightmare:* ICT has shifted from being the experts who had things under control, who battled baddies who wanted to steal our information, who could be trusted to manage a customer's data and information to sharks taking advantage of

the very people who hired or entrusted them with their valuables. Continuous security breaks, hacks, lost and robbed information, manipulation and tracking of our behaviour for the purpose of controlling, steering and making a lot of money. This is ICT's current status: untrustworthy, costly, risky and ethically and morally in a crisis.

ICT service providers, customers and suppliers have the challenge and obligation to not only speak about how awful it is, but to act upon the clear signs of the seriously bad state we are in, as the multiple scandals we read about practically every day indicate. Some parties have taken action, such as the EU with GDPR. It shows it can be done if there is a will, and the courage, to do so.

10. *The disruptive new developments:* The mere fact there is disruption doesn't automatically mean it is something to welcome. Doom scenarios aren't constructive either, but a realistic outlook is never a bad idea. We tend to see the developments as a given and we are encouraged not to question the disruption too much but to jump on the bandwagon. Instead of getting all hyped up about the internet of things, perhaps we could have a look at the psychology of things and add some ethical and moral things into the mix as well. The hyped up Artificial Intelligence could use some Authentic Human Intelligence. That is, after all, the origin of what we put out there and the basis of service provider, customer and supplier interaction. We live in a hyped up world. Social media "helps" us to hype, be hyped up and be in a quasi-permanent state of hyperventilation. We need to calm down, cool off and use our common sense.

11. *(Dis) Trust:* Point five, customer (dis) satisfaction, mentions the special position ICT and big tech companies consider themselves in and the fact this has led to arrogance on many levels. It has also led to hubris. The manner in which many ICT companies and specifically big tech companies speak and the language they employ show their conviction of being the amazing leaders to be followed, at their speed and on their terms of course. Their hubris has led to a delusional perception of their own elevated position in the shaping of life.

However, they are reminded of the financial crises and that trust is what defines the continuity of a business. ICT is no exception, even though they may think so. We are all subject to the same laws. A stark reminder where hubris takes you is from the Greek mythological story of Daedalus and

Icarus: soaring higher and higher towards the sun, not heeding his father's repeated warnings, the melting of the wax which kept the wings together for young Icarus to tragically plunge into the sea and perish.

ICT service providers and big tech had and have many challenges, they organize themselves to face them, they introduce frameworks, methodologies, workflows, etc., to face those challenges but they don't solve or improve anything because the leading force and prevailing attitude to doing business is not designing something well, making something well, delivering something well the first time round but it is about selling something as fast as you can and making money as fast as you can. Quality, robustness and decency is sacrificed, long live the quick buck.

The best way to predict your future is to create it

Peter Drucker

Patience leads to power; but eagerness in greed leads to loss

H.P. Blavatsky

2

The Hallelujah Anglo Saxon Capitalist Model

Money, money, money ... but we do it for the customer!
Winners & Losers, Us & Them
Not humans, but human resources, stupid!
Doing the right thing, right, the first time
Moral split

MONEY, MONEY, MONEY ... BUT WE DO IT FOR THE CUSTOMER!

How have we reached the point where the only driving force in business, as well as in government unfortunately, is money, expressed in the leading principles of economic growth, cost cutting and efficiency and aptly referred to by some as management by Excel?

Generations of students have been taught that economics is the science that studies the allocation of scarce resources, or the science of rational choice. That suggests that economics is about scarcity, and thus about survival in a world where you need and want to overcome hardship with permanent growth, increasing income and more profit. This stems from the Great Depression and in those days made sense considering the difficulties President Franklin Roosevelt faced. His response to the woes were his New Deal, a systematic intervention in what had been a laissez-faire capitalist market economy that had caused the New York Stock Exchange crash in October 1929. The economic crisis influenced economist John Keynes to develop his theory of effective demand which led him, and Roosevelt as well, to create and adopt an accounting system to drive and manage the necessary government interventions.

Our reality is a different one in 2019 however and applying the same methods and approach as in the 1930s doesn't make sense. At least we should question the system, as well as ourselves, and consider if the actions we take on a governmental and/or corporate level are in the general interest of those involved and obtain the desired outcomes.

As for economics being the science of rational choice, it presumes human beings base their decisions on ratio, a cool weighing of pros and cons. It presents life as something that can be rationalized; brought about by science and accounting, expressed with measurements of time, space and production. Just looking at stock market hysterics is enough to dispute that assumption.

Perhaps it is not a bad idea to study, understand and question the foundations and premises on which we base the decisions we make in companies and in governments today. Any company, ICT included, makes decisions based on the balance sheet, the income statement, the cash-flow statement and the statement of retained earnings. These statements came into being as we know them now based on Luca Pacioli's (1447–1517) double-entry accounting system: debit and credit. Double-entry bookkeeping has been accepted as the only complete method of keeping track of and presenting commercial transactions. We accept the numbers presented as trustworthy and a true reflection of the state of affairs of a company or a government. Is that so? How trustworthy are those annual reports packaged in glossy covers? And how trustworthy are the accountant firms who supposedly check those statements of solidity? We accept the annual reports without any questioning and as true. Ah yes, Lehman Brothers, Bank of Scotland, Enron and the accounting auditors Arthur Anderson and Ernst and Young, just to name a few.

Capitalism in its different forms as we know it today but also before being introduced as a term in 1850 by the French politician and historian Louis Blanc in his *Organisation du Travail,* can be linked to double-entry bookkeeping. The following paragraph from Jane Gleeson-White's very informative book *Double Entry* (2011) is interesting and very current:

> The economist Joseph Schumpeter (1883–1950) also traces the develop-ment of capitalism back to double-entry bookkeeping. In *Capitalism, Socialism and Democracy,* published in 1942, Schumpeter says that

capitalism adds a new edge to rationality by "exalting the monetary unit-not in itself a creation of capitalism—into a unit of account. That is to say, capitalist practice turns the unit of money into a tool of rational cost-profit calculations, of which the towering monument is double-entry bookkeeping." In his view, double-entry's cost-profit calculus drives capitalist enterprise—and then spreads throughout the whole culture: "And thus defined and quantified for the economic sector, this type of logic or attitude or method then starts upon it's conqueror's career subjugating—rationalizing- man's tools and philosophies, his medical practice, his picture of the cosmos, his outlook on life, everything in fact including his concepts of beauty and his spiritual ambitions." For Schumpeter, capitalism "generates a formal spirit of critique where the good, the true and the beautiful no longer are honoured; only the useful remains—and that is determined solely by the critical spirit of the accountant's cost-benefit calculation."

Notwithstanding the enormous advantages of quantification and calculus—it helps us to get an overview and somehow be in control of our complex society and business affairs—they have run away with us and have started to live a life of their own. We have reached the point in the twenty-first century where all aspects of life, as Schumpeter writes, are translated extremis into numbers. These numbers are removed from the people, the principles and the values they represent and lead us to a distant observation and mere interpretation of life as a game of calculus. Anno 2019 it is all about algorithms, and we have even reached the point where we celebrate that achievement.

Why is that? That is because a semi-divine quality is given to everything technology related. The registration, gathering of data, linking and (ab)use of it by tech companies is for the benefit of mankind: the all-seeing, all-knowing godlike entities who know best. They are the new rulers of the earth, for our benefit of course, and we should bow to their generosity in spirit of wanting to "take care of us."

The term *evangelist* used in the ICT context is not without reason. We have AI evangelists, plenty of you-name-it-which-technology—evangelists who zealously sell the message of liberation, illumination and smartness. How you can use that term in relation to business and ICT with a straight face is beyond me. What are they implying? The coming of the Messiah clothed in AI robes? The next privacy breaking, private and professional information selling higher entity? Come off your cloud and get real. Please stop preaching your holier-than-thou gospel. No, you are not our savior.

You are a business wanting to make money with ICT. While you're at it, why don't you start with saving yourself first with a bit of inner work and conscience in your business dealings.

The calculation epidemic is visible in the importance given to measurement: if you don't measure it, you don't know it exists. Naturally measuring the progress, performance or compliance of services offered by a service provider is necessary. They have to respect the SLA so that they get paid. But service delivery and support has become KPI (Key Performance Indicators) obsessive. If you comply with KPIs, supposedly you deliver a good service and the customer is satisfied. That is not automatically the case. Customers also have a strong focus on KPIs. Meetings with their counterparts tend to focus practically exclusively on compliance or non-compliance with the defined indicators: Management by KPI. Double-entry bookkeeping and the creativeness used in the various financial statements showing the true state of a company is also applicable to KPIs. One thing is showing a number which indicates a healthy compliance; another thing is how that number was perhaps creatively calculated. I hear less and less customers and service providers speaking about the quality of services received and delivered but hear more and more about the fact whether KPIs have been respected and achieved. All expressed in numbers of course.

The reason I write about double-entry bookkeeping and the Anglo-Saxon capitalist model is because our number focused view of (business) life, expressed in the four types of statements—the balance sheet, the income statement, the cash-flow statement and the statement of retained earnings—have defined and are still defining the decisions we make on business level and how we define our business interactions and our (business) outlook. Our relations as a service provider with our customers, partners, suppliers and last but not least with our own employees has been shaped by a calculus and algorithm focused mindset which a lot of people are not even aware of. The result is what I have described in Chapter 1. It isn't working for us anymore, it is working against us.

A new framework, model or methodology is not going to solve this mindset problem. They are not going to provide better customer satisfaction, a sounder design, a more solid development and delivery on time, within budget and with no errors and bugs as long as the core approach and attitude don't change. They are comparable to band-aids. After a while they come unstuck and then we have to slap on a new one: with a new color, a new form, hoping that they will stay on longer.

To finish this discourse about our root faulty premise on which we base our decisions and which define our *thinking*, our relationships and the leading business dynamic I will cite again a paragraph from *Double Entry*:

> It seems something is fundamentally wrong here. A century and a half of corporate scandals say that financial reporting does not present a reliable picture of corporate wealth and progress, and that auditing does not protect shareholders from manipulative, self-interested managers charged with the care of their assets. Financial statements have failed dismally to reveal the true state of companies whose collapse is a hair's breath away, such as Enron, WorldCom, HIH and One. Tel. They are neither 'transparent' nor 'truthful'. Despite the fact that accounting 'inaccuracies' go hand in hand with sudden corporate collapses and failures, accounting itself is never questioned. Accounting is never held to account. Little has changed since 1933, despite rhetoric, legislation and litigation. The answer how we should account for corporations appears to be as uncertain now as it was eighty years ago.

So here we are in 2019 basing our business decisions as service providers, customers and suppliers on an economic model that uses an unquestioned double entry accounting system which has shown to be limited in scope, easily manipulated and with a sole number and quantification focused perception of business life. This way of thinking is ingrained into our business culture and defines the Bermuda Triangle interactions and relationships we have with our customers, partners, shareholders, stakeholders and employees. We have lived through various financial crises due to the unfettered advance of this thinking and acting; according to analysts we are living in another financial bubble ready to burst. I hope we are not heading for a technological crisis although that might be exactly what we need to shake us out of our unhealthy ICT/technological fantasy world bubble.

Planned Obsolescence is an example of the model gone completely haywire. Obsolescence is described in the Merriam Webster as being in the process of passing out of use or usefulness; becoming obsolete.

We understand that a product becomes obsolete because of the wear and tear. Cars, refrigerators and laptops have to be fixed or replaced at a certain point in time. Obsolescence is part of life, planned obsolescence however, is a different matter and has acquired a whole different charge and implication over time.

The term Planned Obsolescence, as far as we know, was introduced by the American real estate broker Bernard London in 1932 in a pamphlet he wrote called: *Ending the Depression Through Planned Obsolescence.* The 8-page pamphlet makes for interesting reading, not only to understand the term Planned Obsolescence as he defined it but to get a feeling of the times he lived in.

Once again The Great Depression triggered, just as the double-entry bookkeeping adoption and its use on governmental level by Roosevelt and the influence on the ideas of Milton Keynes, another development: Planned Obsolescence. In London's pamphlet we read about classical economics as he dubs it, where the notion is that "the human race was constantly confronted by the spectre of shortages." The danger existed that the growth of population would lead to scarcity of resources. The factories and the farms wouldn't be able to produce enough for everyone. He continues in the next paragraph with, "However, modern technology and the whole adventure of applying creative science to business have so tremendously increased the productivity of our factories and our fields that the essential economic problem has become one of organizing buyers rather than of stimulating producers."

During the Depression, London and his contemporaries considered people had to be stimulated to buy, to consume as much as possible to stimulate the economy. Since enough was being produced, London writes, the consumers had to be organized into buying.

Then he introduces Planned Obsolescence. It worked for the 1930s and got a new boost after WWII in the 1950s during Eisenhower's presidency. The classical economics was replaced by a new "planned obsolescence" focused economic model with its own expressions.

Another name for Planned Obsolescence nowadays is built-in obsolescence and means a policy of planning or designing a product, either in industrial design or economics, with an induced limited useful life, so it will become obsolete after a defined period of time. The objective is to generate long-term sales volume by reducing the time between repeat purchases. This is also known as shortening the replacement cycle. The consequence of this approach is the creation of a lot of waste. The obsolete products with their limited lifespan must be dumped and a new product must be bought. We don't repair products anymore, we are invited to throw them away. Repairing something has nearly become a mission impossible; repair has been made, consciously so, very expensive so as to "stimulate" us to chuck it and just buy a new product.

To understand the whole concept and dynamic of Planned Obsolescence and its impact on our business interactions in 2019 we'll have a look at what the American journalist and social critic Vance Packard wrote and warned about in his book *The Waste Makers* published in 1960. Packard distinguishes three different ways to make a product obsolete:

> ***Obsolescence of function***: In this situation an existing product becomes outmoded when a product is introduced that performs the function better.
> ***Obsolescence of quality***: Here, when it is planned, a product breaks down or wears out at a given time, usually not too distant.
> ***Obsolescence of desirability***: In this situation a product that is still sound in terms of quality or performance becomes 'worn out' in our minds because a styling or other change makes it seem less desirable.

The first type of obsolescence is useful; a camera or glasses with a sharper lens, a quieter air conditioner, a faster train to get us from A to B. We are all in favor of a "genuinely improved product" as Packard rightly states. Unfortunately, the "genuine" aspect tends to evaporate into thin air more and more and is replaced by conscious manipulation to make the product outmoded with the intention of forcing consumers to buy the "improved" version. This ties into the second type of obsolescence, the obsolescence of quality. It is used as a strategy to promote sales and induce, or perhaps a more adequate word is coerce, the consumer to spend his money. In the era of technology, producers as well as consumers know that printers are designed and programmed in such a way that they fail at a predefined moment in time. Or that you are "warned" of cartridges being supposedly empty so please run to the store to buy another one. Luckily ways exist to circumvent this planned failure, at least in regards to the ink issue, but it is tiresome and outright unethical to design a product to fail. Quality has been taken for a ride and shoddiness is the new norm. To make the consumer accept shoddiness and lack of quality, obsolescence of desirability is widely used in the modern era as the new sales and marketing strategy.

You *must* buy the new version of product X because if not, you are out of fashion, you are not modern, you are not in. This is the most powerful type of obsolescence because we, consumers, convince ourselves that we want the new product. Most people are not aware of the fact that producers have fed us the psychological fodder, for us to supposedly arrive all by ourselves at their desired conclusion.

As I write this, in a week's time Apple is launching the next iPhone, or if I believe the rumors and reported leaks, it will launch three new phones. The hysteria and excitement has taken hold of the Apple adepts and although the iPhone they possess at the moment is still working, they will buy one of the new announced models. This is a typical example of obsolescence of desirability. The same psychological conditioning is active in the clothes and shoe fashion world. The dress I wore 6 months ago is out of fashion now so I need to buy the latest trendy outfit if I want to remain desirable. Fashion doesn't exclusively apply to clothes and shoes anymore in the twenty-first century; it applies to technology: to gadgets, to phones, to tablets but also to software, to apps, to social media platforms. Obsolescence of desirability to the hilt. The big advantage for producers is that as a society we are dependent on technology for business and personal activities because everything is being digitized. The replacement cycle is shorter than ever and the producer can keep constant tabs on our habits and track us (wanted and unwanted) and use it to influence our desire for products. We are not talking about obsolescence *in* the mind anymore, a phrase by Packard, but I consider we have reached obsolescence *of* the mind. Devices become smarter, humans are being dumbed down. The device will think for us, so our minds must be switched off. According to the new economic model, we should outsource our discerning minds to "smart" machines.

The new economic model, the Anglo Saxon capitalist model as we know it today, is based on consciously planning, designing and manufacturing products, hardware and software (and services) which will fail at a predestined moment in time so that the consumer must purchase a new product. The model has embraced manipulation of the desires and needs of people with the help of technology. The economic model has been flipped: the consumers are catering to the demand of the producer. The demand for sales … but the customer is king! The best and most deceiving marketing slogan ever.

So if the economic model for your business is based on an as short as possible replacement cycle, it is not surprising that the quality of the product or service is not a priority. Why invest in quality, in making something with added value if it will be discarded within two years? The consumer however needs to have the feeling that he is getting a highly improved device or service, so the producers will throw in a few crumbs—at the least cost possible—and give the consumer the semblance of a major improvement with slick marketing.

Notwithstanding the added value of frameworks and best practices such as ITIL, Lean IT, COBIT, Agile, DevOps etc., they will not solve or make things better in service delivery and support if the root cause of our ineffective and unhealthy relationships, strained communication, questionable service and shoddy products is not addressed. The economic model where the pockets of producers have become the main and total focus point of business decisions and override the need and welfare of buyers of services and products is toxic. Business decisions are based on pushiness, how to make a "user" consume. How to make that user addicted to your product, how to make that consumer pay, again and again for the high of the next gadget. If we are not careful the frameworks, methodologies and models are going exactly down the same road; we invent a new approach which is more holistic, more complete and will make us all a lot happier, won't they? They will "solve" our issues, just wait and see!

The sad part is that there are plenty of people who really care, who want to design and make a well-functioning product which will last, who want to really help a customer, make his day, solve his problem. They don't get the chance; they are being sidelined and end up unhappy and frustrated. More on this topic later in this chapter.

Another impact of the continuous drive for shortening the replacement cycle and focus on speeding up the sales and buying cycle is how training and education in the ICT environment has developed the past 20 years. It has gone from a genuine drive and intention to teach about new best practices, methodologies, standards and frameworks with focus on the content and on quality service delivery to a focus, in my opinion, on diploma obtainment in the shortest time possible, although the volume of the material has increased.

The ICT landscape changes very fast. This requires constant training by ICT professionals to stay up to date and even ahead of developments before they become known to the general public. ICT professionals must be able to answers questions and inquiries made by customers. Apart from giving informed answers and advice they should be able to apply the new developments to their own skill set and work and have the capacity to deliver and support services with the integrated new knowledge.

Our ever growing dependency on ICT for all matters professional (and private) demands, on the service provider's as well as the supplier's and customer's side, sufficient ICT know how to make the correct business decisions and translate the policies to tactical and operational levels. Consequently, training on topics which involve those three levels is necessary.

When ICT started becoming part of the professional world, the main focus was on operational aspects. Of course there is always overlap with tactical issues such as planning and control, but ICT was mostly occupied with making things work and helping the professional when he had a problem. With time this evolved into the more tactical (pre) occupations; not just reactive actions but also attention to pro-active activities. And finally an ICT strategy needed to be developed to manage risks, opportunities and resources for benefit realization.

This development can be traced in the types of training which were developed and the way they are offered. From a service provision perspective, training on how to respond to work interruptions due to ICT problems meant a service desk was crucial and that service incidents were addressed and solved as soon as possible. Introduction of new hardware, modification of existing software or the implementation of a new system implied service providers needed to have processes in place that structured and organized the workflow. And ICT professionals needed to work accordingly. The best practice ITIL came into being and training on, e.g. Incident Management, Change Management, Configuration Management and Service Level Management, etc., took flight. Very early on the scene was the best practice ITIL—you could almost call it the de facto standard for ICT service delivery and support—so I will use it as an example.

ITIL trainings started out with a lot of books, a book per process, but the 2000/2001 version 2 edition had grouped the 10 service management processes and 2 functions into two books: service support and service delivery. The certification scheme, resulting in the highest achievement of obtaining the diploma and title of service manager, consisted of a three day ITIL foundation course with exam to start with.

After the successful completion of the exam, you would continue with a week long course studying the processes and functions described in the service support book and about a month later another five-day course going through the service delivery processes.

The five-day support and delivery courses were taught by two train-ers who would take turns and both courses consisted of numerous group and individual assignments. During those assignments the students were observed and graded by both trainers called an in course assessments on problem analysis, solving problems, creativity, interpersonal sensitivity, personal relations, leadership, delegating/management control, planning/organizing, initiative, perseverance, steadfastness, decisiveness, communi-cation skills and interactive skills to see if they could operate adequately as service managers. After the exercises feedback was given on the above mentioned aspects. For example, presentation skills and communication skills were assessed because for a service manager those skills were fun-damental to be able to perform his responsibilities well. The students had time during the training to improve those skills. If they were weak in cer-tain areas, with the feedback they had received, they could work on them for about a month (or longer) until the second week. On the last day of the second week both trainers, who would discuss every student together and decide on a final grade together, would give the final verdict individually to every participant. If you didn't pass the in course assessment, you were not allowed to do the exam and you wouldn't be able to obtain the certifi-cate of service manager.

The courses were intense, for the students as well for the trainers, inter-active and progressed in an agreeable and manageable pace for all parties involved. You had time to discuss issues that concerned the students, had time to penetrate a topic and had time to give students confidence and support and help them grow. The students had time to digest the informa-tion, to work with the concepts, to improve their presentation and com-munication skills or any other in course assessment topic and to build up confidence in their role as service manager.

Additionally there were practitioner courses. These were hands-on courses to go into the operational details of the individual processes. They prepared, e.g. the change manager to manage in depth the processes he was responsible for.

In 2007 ITIL version 3 was launched. It brought important changes. ITIL is a best practice, so the new ICT developments, challenges for ser-vice providers and lessons learned led to defining the service lifecycle with its five lifecycle stages: service strategy, service design, service transition, service operation and continual service improvement. They consisted of a total of 26 processes and at least 3 functions that help service providers to organize themselves in such a way that they can deliver their services according to the agreed service levels, written down in SLAs. In 2011 an update followed to the current ITIL version 3 to be more complete and even more in tune with the business.

The practitioner courses disappeared however and were replaced by the capability courses: a combination of several processes which were strongly interrelated. These were four-day courses each.

With the implementation of version 3 in 2007, the in course assessments disappeared and the courses were imparted by only one trainer. The format changed from two five-day courses to five three-day courses and include the exam which would be taken on the last day of each course. After completing all the lifecycle courses another three-day course exists called Managing Across the Lifecycle (MALC) to prepare you for the exam using the case which would be presented during the exam itself. The MALC exam is taken and only after a successful score do you obtain the diploma and title of ITIL Expert.

This change meant going from 10 processes taught in 10 days by two trainers, an in-course assessment and two exams (excluding the foundation exam) to obtain the diploma of service manager to 26 processes, introduction of the principles of the 5 lifecycle stages, added sections of lifecycle principles, technology issues and improvement and implementation aspects taught in 15 days by one trainer, another 3 days for exam preparation, no in-course assessment and 6 exams (excluding the foundation exam) to achieve the certification of ITIL Expert.

As you can see, in the version two five-day course, you had more or less a whole day to treat a single process with all associated functions and interfaces with the other processes. In version three, if we take the service design lifecycle as an example you have 8 processes to discuss in 3 days, apart from the section of the lifecycle itself and its principles (a considerable amount), technology considerations and improvement and implementation elements. On the third day the students do the exam. You can imagine the pace, the depth, the discussions and the exercises feasible in that timeframe.

The in-course assessment tested to see if, apart from acquiring the knowledge, you were capable of applying and conveying it. To see if you could act as a service manager and communicate constructively with your colleagues, customers and suppliers. Could you express the issues clearly according to the audience and did you listen just as clearly to what was being said to you? Being an expert in a matter doesn't mean you are an expert in communicating about it with others. Especially so in the ICT world, is my experience. And looking at the problems discussed in the previous chapter related to this topic, there is still work to be done.

Changes are part of life and necessary to make things better but this change makes learning and teaching more difficult. And is the end result the one we intended? I have studied version 1, have taught version 2, version 3 2007 and teach version 3 2011 till the present day and what I see, in all courses I teach at least, is less time to teach more and more and a focus on the single minded zooming in on obtainment of the diploma. This has led to superficiality and to forcing you to teach mainly to prepare for an exam. Additionally, some training institutes even guarantee students passing the exam. The ultimate responsibility to pass an exam is on the student who has to put in the time, effort and dedication to prepare himself adequately. Of course the trainer has to put in her best effort to teach and explain well. But a teacher nor an institute can take responsibility for the attitude, effort and dedicated time to study of a student.

The above-mentioned situation has come into being because students are often put under pressure to pass exams by their own company. The idea is: I am spending money on you, dear employee, so you better give me the ROI (Return On Investment). They use the term ROI but treat it as a cost. The worst thing you can do from a pedagogical and management of change point of view is putting pressure on your people to pass an exam. Another negative influence on the students' frame of mind is adults not being allowed to make mistakes, to fail. Apparently, when you reach the adult age, you know everything and make no mistakes, you can never fail, you understand everything immediately and if not … you are a loser. This is a mentality fed by the quantification and listing of values into the double entry columns described earlier. Which side am I on, the left or the right? The bad or the good? It feeds *on* fear and it *feeds* the fear. More on this topic, the fear factor and its crippling effect, a bit further on in this chapter and more specifically addressed in Chapter 3.

The teacher-student time and interaction is under constant pressure to become the bare minimum. Three days are becoming two. The students are expected to read and study before the course starts (they never do) and are expected to study in the evening, after the course day (they hardly ever do). So there you are on the first day of the two, students haven't prepared, don't have time to study in the evening but they must pass the exam. What are we doing? What is the point? Should institutes even offer courses like this? They do it because their client asks them because there is no time, actually, for training, because the already limited human resources available cannot be missed.

If acquiring new knowledge is so important to the employer and if it is the reason he sends his people to courses; if this new knowledge is the basis of innovation and creation of new business opportunities, full concentration during the training is paramount. Employers have the habit of calling their employees during the course, although they know their employees are occupied. Colleagues do so as well, but will resort more to apping or mail. Where is the logic of enabling your employees to attend a training to subsequently sabotage the learning experience with interruption? Often enough students have had to pull out on the second or third day for an "emergency." The students are "allowed" to learn but must be on call.

Not only the employers or colleagues are doing the—unconscious—sabotaging. The employee could choose to switch off his mobile and not automatically open his laptop when arriving to class to avoid distractions. The teacher will have to protect participants against themselves and set clear house rules regarding electronic devices. In summary, are ICT professionals acquiring the necessary knowledge, do they have sufficient time and is enough depth achieved to be able to add value through the learning experience for the benefit of their company, their customers, themselves? Is this the kind of environment all involved parties want? Does it give all stakeholders the return on investment they need and intended?

According to Gartner survey 2018 CEOs indicated that the most significant internal constraint to growth were employee and talent issues. This was at the top of the list. CEOs said a lack of talent and workplace capability is the biggest inhibitor of digital business progress. Perhaps a critical look at how companies go about their training and knowledge acquirement is in order.

They may claim there are talent and workforce issues, but do their companies have a culture that fosters growth, learning and development? Or is there a culture of fear, fear to fail, to be on the wrong side of the list, to speak up, a culture of no time for anything?

Training and knowledge are evolving into a matter of money and speed as well. If, as we saw earlier, the business decisions and dynamics are principally about shortening the replacement cycle and about focus on speeding up the sales and buying cycle, of training in this case, it is no surprise the quality of training is in danger of becoming secondary.

The service management best practice ITIL was used as an example because it has been around for quite some time and is predominantly present in service providers as a way of working. Customers will ask for service providers to work the ITIL way. What about methodologies or approaches that haven't been around for the same amount of time? Do they get the chance to provide the ICT world with their benefits or are useful best practices and ways of working not taken enough advantage of due to the created dynamics?

Let's have a look at a relatively young twenty-first century way of doing and thinking in the ICT environment: Lean. Lean (manufacturing) has existed since around the thirties of the past century, but the application of the concepts to IT is recent. Lean IT acknowledges the attitude and behavior importance of being more effective and efficient and being more customer focused. The application of Lean to IT gave a whole new way of looking at how services were provided and received by service providers, suppliers and customers. The simple distinction between activities that are value-add (perceived by the customer as adding value and therefore willing to pay for it, such as development of an application), necessary non value-add (work that needs to be done, but does not add value directly for the customer, such as testing the developed application) and non-value add (work which doesn't add any value for the customer, waste, such as rework, bug and error fixing and waiting) was for many already a very useful eye opener. Putting on Lean glasses to look at how your processes (value streams) function, if there is a healthy flow for Just-in-Time delivery and a focus on first time right and quality by preventing defects are all elements which provide considerable advantages, money-wise and in customer satisfaction.

Knowledge and training on Lean and Lean IT can therefore be very beneficial for companies, especially because it addresses those missing aspects, such as Behavior and Attitude, which are the elements that define our customer relations and service delivery so much. It is a shame therefore that the emphasis tends to be so much on a limited view of waste elimination because the core of Lean IT, the people aspect, seems to get buried under the (waste) quantification and classification approach. Once again, the speed and agility which Lean can bring you comes to the fore, and rightly so, but it tends to become center stage and create misbalance by not addressing *all* relevant dimensions in equal measure. We cherry-pick and avoid the confrontational elements.

What has been missing and what service provider organizations ask for currently is help and clarity on how to implement a new methodology, approach or best practice successfully, how to manage the difficult part of

ICT, people, and how to ensure the new way of working sticks and people adhere to it. How to create a culture in your organizations that fosters innovation, creation and development, timely response and problem resolution. It just works and flows.

People, who don't consist of bits and bytes, but who do have, apart from the brains, a heart, are the defining element of any successful enterprise. How do we manage those, and how do we do that in times of change and specifically, in times of permanent swift shifts which require attention and comprehension?

Up till now our way of achieving that is mostly with fine tuning, optimizing and implementing processes or to use another name, value-streams. This is a very necessary aspect to a make sure there is a consistent and healthy (work) flow in your organization which enables it to give the customer what he asks for and needs. There are numerous process oriented best practices, methodologies, etc. The basis of it all, technology, obviously must also work well, be trustworthy and not fall apart too soon. Within the ICT environment we pay plenty of attention to that aspect. People have drifted to the background, were underestimated or taken as a given. They were taken for granted until all the failed projects, disastrous implementations and strained relationships forced ICT to face the fact that management of change implied management of people and giving them considerable attention is necessary if you want those desired changes to add value and enhance your business outcomes.

Frequently (in training) the percentage is given of around 70% of ICT (service management) implementation projects failing due to not enough consideration for the impact of people with their attitude and behavior on the changes. I am unable to verify if this figure is correct, but I do know from my own experience as a service manager and expert in management of organizational change, that yes, the majority of problems and failures can be attributed to the humans. Not because they are a problem, but because ICT organizations focus mostly on processes and technology and in general don't know how to handle the difficult business of people. When we talk about people, we talk about humans on all organizational levels, strategic, tactical and operational.

From a management of change perspective, training on the new methodology you want to implement is *the* moment to obtain commitment and support from your people. It is *the* moment to address the skeletons in the closet, the uncomfortable feelings, people's fears and uncertainties. If you want people to work in a new way and not show resistance, address it, talk about it, give them space to voice their thoughts and feelings. Know and listen to the voice of the customer, in this case of your employees. Many a golden opportunity is lost because the training is merely seen as learning about the new best practice, and not as a way to get your people on board and enthusiastic as well about the new or enhanced way of working. If management on strategic level have decided to implement something new and want their employees to embrace the new framework etc., where are *you*? Why are you never—except in very few cases—in class yourself? Do you already know everything? If you don't (want to) grow as a person and as a professional, how do you expect to foster growth? If you don't want to be led by what you learn, how do you expect to lead and be followed?

We could ask ourselves then, where does that (so called) resistance to change come from? We have accepted as a fact people are resistant to change, they don't like it, they will put up barriers and not permit the much-needed transformation from being successful. Resistance is created when people, the ones who have to change, are not involved, are not informed, are not asked anything.

When their opinions don't matter, when their doubts are perceived as a bother, when their critical observations are considered too uncomfortable. They are a human resource after all and should just get on with it. More on this topic later in this chapter and in the next chapter, the fear factor.

Lean addresses this "people factor" with the Behavior and Attitude dimension and doesn't mince its words about the desired and undesired behaviors if we want to create a constructive atmosphere. So how much attention does this important dimension receive during the various types of training? When we look at the Lean IT foundation courses for example and the order in which the dimensions (Customer, Process, Organization, Performance and Behavior & Attitude) are presented and taught, the Behavior and Attitude dimension, the core of Lean, comes at the end. That also implies, at the end of the course. When people are tired and want to go home. Or getting really nervous because they have to do the exam after the break.

It is understandable to present material going from the known to the unknown. To start with customer, performance, etc. and end with the most unknown and untreated facet, people. But the danger is this dimension only gets superficial attention. The message is lost, its value add is lost. That 70% of failed implementations won't change this way.

Looking at another methodology, COBIT 5 addresses the people aspect in two of its seven enablers of its holistic approach: Culture, ethics and behavior and People, skills and competencies. The fact these two enablers exist at all and are mentioned means the awareness is there that these are fundamental aspects to achieving success for business outcomes. But once again, how much attention do these enablers get during training and when will the direly needed guides on those enablers be published?

COBIT 5 highlights the necessity to implement a change in the correct way. The correct way implies managing the before mentioned enablers; you could say, all things human. Buy in and commitment from all stakeholders are crucial for success as they state in their Implementation guide. COBIT 5 includes the Implementation Life Cycle consisting of three areas of interest: the inner ring of the lifecycle, the Continual improvement lifecycle, the middle ring, Change Enablement and the outer ring, Programme management.

The middle ring, Change Enablement, directly addresses the human, behavioral, cultural aspects and potential barriers when implementing, in this case, the Governance of Enterprise IT. Communication plays a vital part in all the seven phases of this implementation Life Cycle ring. The part on Change enablement states: "In many enterprises, there is not enough emphasis on managing the human, behavioural and cultural aspects of the change and motivating stakeholders to buy into the change."

As we can see, there is a guide for implementing change and the factors which have to be considered., in this case related to GEIT (Governance of Enterprise IT). In regards to training; is the format of three days enough to teach the knowledge required to implement a change and manage a transformation? The quality of the learning experience of a new approach or methodology, as we saw before, is not ideal; the way it has developed and is developing is, in my opinion, too heavily focused on obtaining the certificate. When we are talking about complex matters such as culture, behavior and communication and how defining they are for the success of the transformation, the question is if the time, format and focus on the exam provide the students and their companies with what they need.

In summary, do we get the maximum value out of the experience and will it help us? To be clear, I am not questioning the content and structure of COBIT 5, on the contrary, but I am questioning the way we go about training.

The pressure of having to do the exam immediately, the amount of material and the accelerated pace needed to cover all topics takes the pleasure and the necessity away from studying, from investigating, from trying to figure something out. This translates itself into the manner we do our jobs. We give and receive no time to penetrate the core of an issue, to investigate, to sit back and think with our feet on the table gazing out of the window, to make well-informed decisions. In school, at university or at any other educational institution we go to class, read, study and after some time we do the exam and (hopefully) pass. In ICT we don't do that. We attend the class, do the exam on the last day and obtain the diploma. We are delivering products based on a system which has the churning out of products and services as fast as possible as a basis and this approach is taking over the ICT training environment as well: organizational fast food for instant satisfaction.

We are jumping from one methodology to the other trying to solve an issue when it comes down to being more thorough, consistent, persevering in the ones we are already working with and paying more attention to people. We all know about processes, value streams, workflows or whatever we want to call them; what is needed is insight, awareness, emphasis on what is causing the problems we face and training in the "people" aspect. Perhaps training in not yet another methodology, focused on increasing the speed of actions, but in a dose of basic psychology, group dynamics, in management of organizational change is what we need to make things better and smarter (and make customers satisfied).

The multiple methodologies—I only named a few—can offer considerable added value to service providers, suppliers and customers when facilitated in the right environment. The learned knowledge permits employees to create, innovate and make things work better and more efficient. The continuous drive for shortening the replacement cycle and the focus on speeding up of all of our activities, including training, undermines, as I see it, what we are trying to achieve.

When mentioning the tunnel vision focus on speed and money the reaction is often a shrugging of shoulders and the announcement that it is what it is, it is how things progress, that is what is happening—it is happening *to* us—and there is nothing we can do about it. We have to live with it; a service provider says: the customer wants it, we have to cater to them. The customer says: the new ICT developments force us to adopt these new technologies and systems because otherwise we will not be competitive. The supplier says: all these new technologies make your lives better so we just offer those possibilities for the benefit of all. We have no responsibility in the dynamic created, we are on the receiving end of "developments" and it is either us or them. If you can't beat them, join them.

Convenient, isn't it? Let's throw our hands up in the air and proclaim we have nothing to do with it, we have no power over our (business) destiny. Planned obsolescence of quality and desirability and "the market" define our direction, let's go along for the ride.

WINNERS & LOSERS, US & THEM

The double entry accounting system we have adopted for our finances and administration and specifically the quantification of those entries has made its way into all dimensions of business life, not only the financial one. Decisions are based on items we have registered either on the left or on the right as numbers and/or percentages. We think in twos: credit-debit and profit-loss. There is a beginning and an end. There is a problem and then a solution. Cause and effect. We think in twos.

Duality is part of life. It's definition according to Merriam Webster is: the quality or state of having two parts. There is no value judgment related to those two parts. Humans pass a judgment by preferring one over the other, considering one is bad and the other good. That way, we apply a separation in our thinking and this expresses itself in our doing (and feeling for that matter). Taking the temperature of water as an example: hot and cold. There is no good and bad there. Only a preference, according to the circumstances and your preferences. If there is a blistering sun, you prefer a cool drink and in winter with the cold, you will prefer a hot drink. Variation is possible when the two "opposites" come together. Warm water, lukewarm water, etc. Colder or hotter according to the amount of hot or cold water you pour into the mix. Creation with all its possibilities and nuances is achieved with the meeting of opposites. Life itself is created that way, a child is born.

In the color spectrum, black and white are considered opposites. They just are, there is no inherent good or bad in the colors. When we apply our preference, which is totally subjective, we can consider black good and white bad, or vice versa. In some countries they dress in black when attending a funeral, in other countries they dress in white.

In Scandinavian countries, where the winter is long and dark, white is a popular color for interior design. It enhances the little light there is during winter. Staying in the Nordic regions, the Aurora Borealis can lighten the nights and thick curtains to keep the light out are needed to be able to sleep.

On and on we can go. Tall-short, thick-thin, hard-soft. Introvert-extrovert, fast-slow, left-right, positive-negative (charged) energy. Duality exists. The two elements of duality simply are. They are in a state of being. When you put a seed in the earth, it needs the moist and the dark to sprout and then make its way to the light for further nourishment. Both the dark and light are needed to help the plant grow and give fruit. Or speed: sometimes you must accelerate or slow down because something happened. You might have to swerve left or right to avoid a crash, accelerate to ensure a safe crossing or brake and regroup before continuing. Things happen, circumstances ask for a reaction, but humans add a value judgment with their preferences and expectations.

When we add the preference, apply a judgment and consider that it is the truth and the "right" way we enter the terrain of thinking in better versus worse. It is easy to make the step to superior and inferior, us and them, winners and losers. We split our thinking with the judgment we pass. We split it even more when we lose the link to the object due to quantification, because we convert it into an abstract concept. It is a number. There is a desire to classify our reality with duality because it makes our life, or so we think, easier to manage. Due to quantification of duality, we can compare the numbers and there you are, the decision to be weighed is made easier.

Apart from a fixation on numbers, and in extension on money, the dual thinking leads to the us and them view with the associated better/worse or superior/inferior attitude which creates difficult and awkward communications and relations with our stakeholders, as described in Chapter 1. Not only do these difficulties exist between the exterior stakeholders but they also exist *within* the same organization. The following real life example illustrates this.

A long lasting and complex project had been accomplished successfully. The company consisted mainly of people of two nationalities, representing the partners of the joint venture but other nationalities were also part of the team. Management decided to organize an activity with all people involved who put in a lot of extra hours and sweated to make it happen. A lunch in a picturesque setting was organized.

The restaurant consisted of multiple round tables which seated up to seven people. There was no formal seating plan, so we were all free to take a seat where we pleased. And so we did. There was one exception. Management were all sitting at the same table. The message this conveyed was very clear. Us and them.

The people at the table consisted of management from the two partners and an important supplier. The partners didn't interact; they spoke their own languages and had their own conversations, ignoring the other party completely. Nobody made any effort to involve the whole table in one conversation or to involve anyone from the other partner. Us and them at the same table.

At no time did management—except one—mingle with the occupants at the other tables, the people who had worked very hard for years and months to ensure success. They were the other "side": them.

This attitude and behavior was representative of the dynamics on the work floor and illustrated the type of communication and relationships the company had with its customers and suppliers as well.

The us & them expanding like an oil slick: At the table, in the restaurant, on the work floor, between management and employees, between service providers and customers and between suppliers and service providers. The us *and* them quickly translates to us *versus* them. It is no surprise communication within companies often does not flow. Let alone when interacting with other parties. Customer satisfaction?

When we add the capitalist Anglo Saxon solely-money-oriented-approach to (business) life to the mix it leads to thoughts of winners and losers. As if life is a competition … competing against others … what's the prize …? Money? The old Greek come to mind when participating at the Olympics. Their prize was honor and a laurel wreath. They competed for the satisfaction, pleasure and honor to measure themselves against others. Perhaps it is no coincidence that only men were allowed to participate. There seems to be a constant need for competition and coming out on top. And being able to label a person or a group of people losers seems to give great satisfaction. Indeed it does … to the ego. The ego does need to be fed continuously after all.

Winning business is great and naturally companies want to be successful. They will do all in their power to make the best proposal to convince the customer their offer is what the customer needs. But doing it the way we are doing it now, however, in the twenty-first century, with less resources, less time, less interest in quality for the sole purpose to win more and more money, faster and faster is a "the end justifies the means" dynamic which is having serious repercussions on business and people's health.

This thinking in twos, in cause and effect, how we get from A to B to solve a problem goes hand in hand with what we call linear thinking. Linear thinking puts order in a reality in a sequential manner, as a straight line. Issues are addressed and solved going from step 1, to step 2, to step 3, etc. We have been taught to analyze a problem by breaking it down into its constituent parts to understand it. That means we separate into individual items the object of our study. Analysis signifies separation of a whole into its component parts. We break down a complex situation to obtain better comprehension. Figure 2.1 shows the separate steps we take, or the separate activities of a process we follow, to obtain our goal.

Figure 2.1 will be recognizable as a typical process flow resulting in the output, the end result depicted as E. The output of a car factory is a built car, the output of a cookie factory packaged cookies and of the change management value stream an implemented change. The value stream steps A to D, executed in a specific chronological order leads to the final outcome E.

System think or a systemic approach on the other hand means you look at an individual element but always put it in the context of a whole and are aware, or do your utmost to understand, how the various elements interrelate, and how they are interdependent. You can zoom in on an element but will always zoom out again to have the broad overview, to understand the system with all its actors. Let's have a look at the following examples, starting with the most impressive system of all, the human body.

The human body is an excellent example of a sophisticated system where all the independent elements are interrelated, interdependent and where the nonfunctioning or ill organ will have an impact on the whole being, on the whole system. Spots or rash on your face or back is an indication the system, the body, is out of sync and does not mean it is solely a "face" problem because the spots are on the face, or a back problem because the rash is located on the back. The symptoms appear somewhere on the body, the root causes can be multiple or intensified by other bodily conditions: types of food, time of food intake, hygiene of the food preparation, allergies,

FIGURE 2.1

A linear approach to achieve results. The desired end-result E is achieved when we apply a structured and disciplined approach and break up the journey into individual items, starting with step A, then B, C and D.

condition of immune system, bodily hygiene, stress, living conditions etc. A systemic approach takes all these factors into account and examines which factors and how these influence the body with the spots or rash as a result.

A company is a system as well, with multiple elements and actors which are interrelated and interdependent. Only focusing on the processes, as we tend to do, is not enough. Yes, we zoom in on a process and fine tune or optimize it, which certainly is helpful, but the process is only a part of all the elements in an organization which see to it the company achieves its business outcomes. We tend to forget to zoom out and take time to take a critical look at the overall picture. Other elements to consider which contribute to achieving the business outcomes are the organizational structure, culture, management information systems and tooling, skills of people, their roles and responsibilities, attitude and behavior, decision making structure, ethics, IT architecture, customers, suppliers, partners, types of contracts, etc.

Figure 2.2 illustrates the above mentioned situation. There are multiple factors which have an influence on the (business) end result. The box with (D) depicts the end result of a process, e.g. the change process. D is an implemented change. The implemented change enables the customer to achieve its business outcomes, represented as E. The implemented change enables the bank to offer its online services and sell its products. But not only the change process with a successful implemented change contributes to the bank being able to offer its products to its customers as the former paragraph stated with the body example. The boxes with I, II,

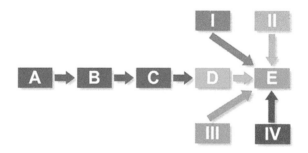

FIGURE 2.2

A more complete view of business dynamics. A holistic approach and systemic view of business dynamics, meaning the multiple elements influencing business interactions are taken into account, will enable organizations such as service providers to respond adequately to customer demand and obtain customer satisfaction.

III and IV are the other facets influencing the bank being able to sell its products and services such as ethics, skills of people, etc.

Mentioning the other elements in an organization doesn't make it holistic, however. It is a first step but the identification of those other elements, relationships and interdependencies, *understanding* them, and *acting* upon them is what holistic truly is. That is the systemic approach.

In the ICT world the non-systemic approach to implementations of for instance ITIL or COBIT has caused many failures and problematic situations, frequently with an undesired end result. People often get a fit just hearing the word COBIT or ITIL uttered. I have been involved in quite a few projects where that is the case and to turn around a situation like that is not easy, apart from the frustration for the people involved.

Organizations, when there were problems with an implementation or when they have gone through a failure, still tend to go about the new implementation in the same way. They then think the processes were not described adequately, or the roles were not defined in enough detail etc. but they usually don't look hard enough why the initial project failed, what came even before that. Lays offs, a lost big deal, an unpleasant work environment can impact the success of a project in a negative way if not handled well or insufficiently understood and addressed. Or perhaps there is a culture of repercussion and nobody dares to speak up. Many an organization suffers from trauma they are not aware of. If we don't understand that, we could repeat the same mistakes, again and again. Linear thinking simplifies the complex reality we have to understand, manage and oversee too much and consequently makes us miss important aspects or misdirect our energy.

It is not a matter of either-or. Linear thinking as well as systemic thinking are useful. But they must be combined to ensure we gain enough knowledge about the situation at hand. Analysis of the multiple elements involved in systemic thinking must be done with sufficient depth as well. The linear way of thinking and specifically the way we do it now, stays on the surface due to the hurry we are always in; apart from not considering all elements from the beginning. The systemic approach however, when we adopt it, must also be careful to not stay on the surface but must dig a little deeper. We need both breadth and depth. That is what ICT people perhaps need to really be able to understand the customer.

In depth expertise is necessary but knowledge in breadth, meaning understanding down to a certain level and placing ICT and your activities within the bigger context, understanding the relationships and interdependencies only make you stronger and more able and capable to service your customers. Only an in depth knowledge and approach is as if you have blinders on; permit yourself to have a broader, more interrelated view.

People working in ICT tend to see the world through bits and bytes glasses and speak about rollouts, fallbacks, etc. It is a linear way of working. A project involving a new way of working, the introduction of any kind of framework, whether you call it holistic or not, implies taking people, ergo culture, into account. The mindset, attitudes and behavior must all be considered and addressed when wanting to change or transform aspects of your organization. You cannot "roll out" a change or transformation when culture is involved, which is always. That is the reason why so many change projects fail in the ICT world. And elsewhere for that matter.

It is also the reason why so many companies focus on acquiring and rolling out a new tool because implementing a tool is manageable and can be approached in a linear way. Unfortunately, they soon discover that the tool is not the magic solution and what actually makes the change or transformation successful is not the tool but the mindset and thus behavior of the people who have to work with the tool. They go about it in the wrong order as well. First they buy the tool and then the workflows are adapted to those tools instead of defining first how you want to work to achieve a specific outcome and *then* looking for the instrument that will help you obtain the result you have defined. A lot of money, effort, frustration and strained relations could be avoided.

To understand the linear way of thinking and the effect on organizations, the development and history of the human being, body and science can help. A linear line of approach is treating the human body as a machine that can be fixed. The broken part is isolated, we zoom in on what is not functioning and try to make it better, or sometimes remove it altogether. The machine metaphor was introduced in the early 1600s by the French philosopher René Descartes. The emergence of science as we know it today which began in those days changed vitalism with scientific materialism. Industrial revolution consolidated the machine approach to the human body.

To understand what vitalism is, I quote from the article *Vitalism* by William Bechtel and Richardson, Robert C. The summary of the article as it appears in the Routledge Encyclopedia of Philosophy begins as follows:

> Vitalists hold that living organisms are fundamentally different from non-living entities because they contain some non-physical element or are governed by different principles than are inanimate things. In its simplest form,

vitalism holds that living entities contain some fluid, or a distinctive "spirit." In more sophisticated forms, the vital spirit becomes a substance infusing bodies and giving life to them; or vitalism becomes the view that there is a distinctive organization among living things. Vitalist positions can be traced back to antiquity … Vitalism is best understood, however, in the context of the emergence of modern science during the sixteenth and seventeenth centuries. Mechanistic explanations of natural phenomena were extended to biological systems by Descartes and his successors. Descartes maintained that animals, and the human body, are 'automata', mechanical devices differing from artificial devices only in their degree of complexity. Vitalism developed as a contrast to this mechanistic view. Over the next three centuries, numerous figures opposed the extension of Cartesian mechanism to biology, arguing that matter could not explain movement, perception, development or life.

There is ongoing discussion on the topic.

Professor of Life Sciences at *Arizona State University*, Randolph Nesse in his 2009 article *What will change everything* states: Replacing the machine metaphor with a more biological view of the body will change biology in fundamental ways. The transition will be difficult because the metaphor of body as machine has served us well. It sped escape from vitalism, and encouraged analyses of the body's components, connections, and functions, as if they were the creations of some extraordinarily clever cosmic engineer. It has yielded explanations with boxes and arrows, as if the parts are components of an efficient device. Thanks to the metaphor of the body as machine, vitalism has been replaced by an incredible understanding of the body's mechanisms.

Now, however, genetic advances are revealing the metaphor's limitations. For instance, a decade ago it was reasonable to think we would find the genes that cause bipolar disease. New data has dashed these hopes. Bipolar disease is not caused by consistent genetic variations with large effects. Instead, it may arise from many different mutations, or from the interacting tiny effects of dozens of genes." To continue with the machine metaphor as an example of flawed linear thinking applied to a system, he continues:

Dozens of genes, hormones and neural pathways influence each other in interactions that defy description, even while they do what needs to be done. We have assumed, following the metaphor of the machine, that the body is extremely complex. We have yet to acknowledge that some evolved systems may be indescribably complex … Indescribable complexity does, however, confront us with the inadequacy of models built to suit our human preferences for discrete categories, specific functions, and one directional causal arrows. Worse than merely inadequate, attempts to describe the body as a machine foster inaccurate oversimplifications. Some bodily systems cannot be described in terms simple enough to be satisfying; others may not be described adequately even by the most complex models we can imagine.

This last paragraph can read as the organizational body, the organizational system approached and treated as a machine despite the fact that it is an ever evolving and complex system with many interdependencies. The models we use to get a grip on and understanding of that high complexity entails a "system" model, or in other words a holistic, interrelated model which represents the systemic complexity in an adequate manner; which enables us to achieve an as trustworthy and correct as possible representation of that complex reality. If we want trustworthy information so we can make well informed and effective decisions we need to adopt a more systemic approach to how organizations function.

Within organizations, a non-systemic way of thinking is not explaining and not showing people on operational level where and how they fit into the big picture of the company. Just do the work, we, on strategic and tactical level will do the thinking. We expect people on operational level to run and get things done but we are not willing to make the effort to show them how it all fits together. The reasoning and the literal words I have heard uttered are: they don't need to know. As in: they are a mere cog in the wheel. It is irrelevant they understand. What is actually being said is: *they* are irrelevant. And the addressed in this way know you mean that. And then, surprise … there is resistance regarding this new way of working management wants to introduce. Where on earth would that resistance have come from?

There are methodologies and best practices, the ones normally called holistic, which make an attempt to approach the organizational system as such, with a systemic focus. They can be recognized by paying attention to more than to the mere processes which need to flow. They focus just as much on people as on technology and value streams. And when implementing a new framework, methodology or best practice a systemic approach should be used to ensure success. An organization can have the best technology and wonderful work, information and communication flows on paper, but in the end, it is the quality of the people which make the system work.

Another duality which has presence in our (business) interactions is inside-outside or internal-external. We are very busy with the outside and are not aware, ignore or avoid the inside.

Our attention is to the outside world, to our customers including the new potential ones, to our suppliers, to the "markets." The "inside" attention is how we can organize our company in such a way we achieve the business outcomes we want. Currently we do that by focusing primarily on value streams and processes but this is too limiting. What about the inside focus on ourselves? Do we observe and analyze ourselves, being active either on strategic, tactical or operational level? Do we understand how we influence the environment and how we fit into the overall system?

When we focus so heavily on the outside world, what do we see? What do we project into and onto that world? Our assumptions, preferences, dreams, desires and demands are part of our package and mindset which is put out there when we interact with our customers and employees. How aware are we of this projection? Are we happy with it, and with its effect and impact? Do we even realize we are projecting?

We are often surprised and uncomfortable with the fact that the relationships and communication between service providers, customers and suppliers are so difficult and tense. We encounter difficulties and resistance from our colleagues and employees. The ongoing shortening of the sales cycle and of the replacement cycle have us in its grip and are, quite frankly, making everyone unhappy. People cannot design and make beautiful and qualitatively solid products anymore, have no time for it, get no time for it, are stressed out, get burn-out, stop enjoying their work and the majority doesn't even get the salary to make it worthwhile.

NOT HUMANS, BUT HUMAN RESOURCES, STUPID!

For Schumpeter, quoted from Gleeson-White's *Double Entry*, capitalism "generates a formal spirit of critique where the good, the true and the beautiful no longer are honored; only the **useful** (my highlight) remains-and that is determined solely by the critical spirit of the accountant's cost-benefit calculation."

The human in organizations is also perceived and treated as a resource. Useful and expressible in numbers which you can add and subtract. An employee is a resource, "its" worth measured in the same way as hardware, software, furniture and cars. Consequently, they are just as disposable. However, there is a small problem with this resource. They think, they feel, they can disagree. You cannot read their minds, predict their reactions. Some have morals and principles. They are unpredictable and un-programmable. And since optimal performance is crucial in the Anglo Saxon capitalist efficiency-speed-money scheme employees have to be molded into perfect money making machines. The employee is a resource and too human characteristics can imperil the business objectives. That's why we like the potential of AI so much.

When we do address the human element in an organization the approach is primarily on how to enhance the output of that human resource and how to avoid those human resources showing resistance or any kind of unwelcome behavior when there are changes. Again we have the linear approach which is a reason why transformation initiatives or projects within organizations fail. Treating humans as human beings instead of resources with their multiple dimensions, considering their good, bad and ugly entails a psychological view and comprehension of that complex system which starts with psychological awareness and insight into your own complex interior. For the majority of people that prospect is very scary because you are confronted with yourself, not only with your good side, but also with your shadow side. Our self-image can get in the way or we can simply not accept any questioning of the image we have of ourselves or the one we project into the world. But as long as we are not conscious of those psychological dynamics and how our behavior is defined by them, the greater the chance of failed relationships and interactions with our employees, customers and suppliers and the greater the chance of failed transformation projects, even though we call them digital. Being scared of the human factors is being scared of yourself.

Planned Obsolescence of Humans

The fascination with robots and artificial intelligence is not a coincidence. The more complex and troublesome our world, the less we see and are capable of penetrating the system with its multiple interactions, the more we crave control and order to make sense of our reality. We have created a world where the value of our life is expressed in how much we own and how we spend it. We think we can achieve the desired control, order and ownership with technology. Many have given technology the power to define their destiny and worthiness.

Tools and instruments are what their names imply: tools and instruments. To help us, human beings, perform tasks better, faster, more precisely and cheaper. These tools and instruments, such as technology, are at the service of mankind to give us value-add and benefits for a healthy, pleasant and productive life. But that has changed. We are shifting to the reversed order of humans servicing technology and their manufacturers. By giving machines and robots more human characteristics, supposedly thinking and feeling, and eliminating or phasing the human characteristics out of the humans and giving them more machine-like elements: chips in the body, enhanced reality glasses, etc. We are requested, no, I should say, *pushed* to desire, to be more like machines. We are desiring our own obsolescence and are naively going along with it.

Outrageous? We are already doing it and we are already treating people as performance focused machines with less and less regard for their human being-ness. Work overtime is becoming the norm, not the exception, work in weekends is not seen as a no-no anymore, availability (thanks to tech) at any time, is practically imposed. You are visible, you are trackable, with or without your consent, you *are* tracked, continuously. For what? To work, to consume and to be held in check.

AI, robots and the like are putting "human" aspects to the machine resource because they are much easier to manage, much easier to control, much easier to do away with. And the people? They are spoon fed distractions such as enhanced reality or augmented reality glasses; augment and enhance? Augment with what? What for? Better to call it augmented fantasy. Nothing to do with reality but all to do with virtuality. Escaping from reality and blurring it with artificial elements but pretending it is "real." Who are you trying to mislead? Here we are happily skipping into an artificial fantasy world where we are our own super heroes.

Augmented reality and the gadget and app over-orientation distract us from ourselves. It "helps" us to not reflect, to not question, to not contemplate, to not discern. It "helps" us to not go within.

It "helps" us to not project our fears, worries and faults into the world and onto others, but to project a wonder world where we are the heroes in our own made up story. In other words, augmented/enhanced reality glasses are an effective tool for escapism and for keeping the human being distracted.

Social media is often used as a distraction from ourselves as well. It invites us to consume and not to think. It invites us to react like Pavlov's dog, not to think independently and critically. It elevates lemming behavior to a desirable state because we "like" and "follow." Another beautiful example of obsolescence of desirability. Dumbing down the human being with the purpose for it to be a mere resource in the grander scale of things, scaling up the "humanness" of machines. And the human resources clap on the sidelines for these astonishing developments and "progress." Are all uses of social media questionable? Of course not, but the human being tends to go from the use of a tool to the abuse of it with astonishing speed and gullibility.

This is the reality we are creating and the culture we propagate. Within organizations the leaders and managers define the dominant culture and their attitude, behavior and their decisions create, enable and enhance the desired culture.

With the organizational principles and policies the rules of the game are implemented. Does the organizational culture of a service provider enhance and enable customer satisfaction? Does it enhance and enable a way of working, the work ethic leaders and managers desire? For the benefit of the organization, for the customer, the employee, the partner? In summary, for all stakeholders? One thing is a lofty vision statement and mission; another is acting accordingly. Do leaders and managers practice what they preach?

If service providers are interested in holistic frameworks and methodologies and see the sense in paying more attention to multiple principles and enablers (COBIT 5) or dimensions (lean IT) to ensure the service delivery and support they want and need to provide, they will understand that goes hand in hand with a more holistic leadership as well. Holistic leadership implies a different kind of intelligence, the emotional one. You can only have emotional intelligence if you are in touch with your own emotions and when you are aware of their workings. Only with awareness and balance with yourself is it possible to lead others intelligently.

Lean and the motto of Toyota's chairman Cho comes to the forefront again: Go See, Ask Why, Show Respect. The third principle, Show Respect, which implies listening, offers enough challenge to plenty of leaders and managers as it is.

Listening is not just hearing with your ears and listening with your mind, but includes "listening" to the non-verbal communication, such as facial expressions, body language and silence. A lot can be said with silence. And a lot can be heard in silence. Listening is strongly tied together with the second Cho principle, Show Respect. If you are not an active listener it is a sign of disrespect; you are not in the moment, paying attention to the person in front of you, but absorbed in other activities. Your mind wanders off while the person is speaking or you are busy with your own reaction instead of just absorbing what is being said. The shame is you miss a lot of information which can prove very important for decision making.

Dr. Erik van de Loo, Affiliate Professor of Organizational Behavior at INSEAD contributed to the book by *Manfred F.R. Kets de Vries. Coach and Couch: The Psychology of Making Better Leaders* (2nd edition, 2016) with an article called *The Art of Listening*. In his conclusion he states:

> We have explored the essential processes and dynamics of listening. The art of listening from a clinical perspective is to listen below the surface. It is the art of being open and sensitive to unconscious levels of meaning and to more archaic levels of experiencing. In order to be able to access these in others, one must be capable of accessing them in oneself. Mentalizing (understanding that human behavior is caused by various and varying states of mind) is a necessary but insufficient precondition for listening. Empathy and intuition are valuable ways of connecting with out-of-conscious levels of meaning and experience. As such, they are important tools for data collection.

The following paragraph also makes for interesting reading and functions as a useful reminder: "Listening is an interpersonal situation that takes place in a relationship. The relationship can be described on various levels (real relationship, working alliance, and counter-transference) … We are advised to listen with a mind as open as possible and with free-floating attention. If possible, we should listen without memory or desire. But we must acknowledge that a neutral or empty mind is an illusion; our minds are full of concepts, thoughts, and frameworks. Self-decentered listening is a more realistic ambition."

And to top it off: "Listening to others presupposes and incorporates listening to oneself. The other, and his or her narrative, resonate in oneself. At times the listener is like an emotional mirror for the other."

The following personal experience illustrates the above. Part of a project I was involved in included training the organization on a new framework and approach to service delivery and support. This new way of working and structuring activities were important for compliance with the contract. All the relevant people had been trained and the only people missing were the managers on strategic and tactical level. The training totaled 3 days, but management didn't have the time so it was reduced to two … and then to one. I had one day to give them the background and approach and to explain how it was adopted to their organization. It was not straightforward and rather complex.

The morning started with the explanation of the methodology. The idea was to give them sufficient knowledge to enable them to understand how it had been adapted to their particular situation since it was the foundation on which their framework was built. This would give them a clear picture what this way of working would mean for their people and the impact it would have. Within half an hour I was losing their attention. They wanted to get to the tailoring of the approach to their company. So I stopped what I was doing and showed them their framework. I explained I would walk them through it so they would understand. It was an impossible feat. I was constantly interrupted, got comments about what was missing or what should have been different and when trying to explain, I was interrupted again. The people present started discussing the framework among themselves, made the wrong conclusions and didn't listen when I tried to correct them. Only one person present asked questions and made a real effort to understand what he was seeing and hearing.

I remember being rather amazed at what played out in front of me and was left wondering how they would understand what was going on in their organization in relation to service delivery and support and how they would understand their employees if they didn't know how it worked. They didn't listen, apparently immediately "knew" everything and also immediately had an opinion. They took no time to digest the information, or have a constructive discussion about it. I really wondered how they were going to make well-informed decisions regarding this topic. It is easy to fall into this pitfall of not listening; I have to be on the alert as well and have fallen often enough. A big lesson learned. However, we may expect leaders and managers to have the emotional intelligence to navigate these waters, especially considering the mark they make on organizational culture and on the future of the company. And more so when they trumpet their opinion so explicitly. Unfortunately I encounter this sort of behavior frequently and observe it just as often. It influences what is described in Chapter 1 about the communication and the information flows which don't always flow but stagnate.

Cho's Show Respect has many facets but is actually quite simple. Treat another the way you want to be treated is what it boils down to. It implies you approach another person with genuine interest and with an authentic openness for dialogue and understanding. It implies putting yourself in the position of the other and being able to relate. It implies not going on the defensive, nor the attack, not needing to show who is boss because you are insecure and your ego needs a boost.

Showing respect is looking people in the eye when you speak to them (although in some countries you shouldn't so consider the cultural context), giving them the time to do their work or have their say, not interrupting them when they speak, not making someone put a lot of effort into a presentation and then disregarding it, or asking for last minute changes because you changed your mind. Showing Respect is having a decent coffee machine, giving people their credit, not coming late to meetings and being organized. Showing Respect is showing your face on the work floor, not only when you *want* something but because you are interested to know how things are. Respect is considering people's private space and holidays and not interrupting them when they are in class.

What about Ask Why? People in organizations are adults and professionals. They will do things for a reason. Ask them. Not only once but several times. Asking only once, disagreeing with the answer and then proffering your own opinion doesn't always penetrate to the root of the matter. Why did they do what they did? Why did they use that model, why did they structure the activities in that way, why did they involve those people and why not these others? Why didn't you come to me when you had a problem? And when employees ask managers why? Are managers able and willing to give an answer?

When we look at Mr. Cho's simple but to the point principles we can conclude they are not as common as they should be. Are these three principles present within companies and do they influence the organizational culture? And if they are not, why?

An organization is a system and the system will do all in its power to survive. Organizations have an auto immune system which means they will "attack" or render helpless the rogue element or the element which doesn't conform to the system. We hire people who fit into the system and get rid of those who don't.

Organizational culture keeps the system functioning as it should, it maintains the cultural status quo. Leaders and managers might define the culture and set the tone, employees make sure the culture is kept intact as was defined and as is expressed. "This is the way we do things here" fits into that mindset.

Employees criticize their management for all kinds of reasons but they are complicit to an organizational culture when they sustain that potentially unhealthy organizational culture, when they don't question it and when they copy the very behavior they criticize. People often say it is difficult to question or criticize management because it can influence their career in a negative way. This fear to disagree, question and ask why is addressed in Chapter 3, the Fear Factor. Fear is very much part of many companies and their culture; it creates a downward spiral in attitude, behavior and ethical business dealings.

There are also employees who see their top management as some sort of hero who will solve all problems, who knows best and who cannot fail. Leaders somehow need to be dressed in a cape and transformed into superman, often with great need for applause.

A business has to be managed well, with a team of individuals with their respective expertise to get the job done. All stakeholders must be on the same page and it should be a pleasure to do your part well and enjoy the successes. A business doesn't need hero worship and unconditional loyalty to the superhero of the moment. Hero worship is outsourcing responsibility for yourself and your actions to another, with all related implications.

In ICT hero worship is high. Apart from the dedication to the CEO and/ or founder of the company, the product itself is venerated. The person as well as the product is hyped as most extraordinary and the solution to a so called customer demand. The planned obsolescence of quality and desirability strategy has made us, apart from fooling us into desiring something new continuously we are willing to fork out a lot of money for, into clap cattle for the "leader" of these companies. We adore and admire the leader because it takes away any uncomfortable feeling we could have and it takes away the need to have a (hard) look at yourself; at what you wish, what you live for, what you think, feel and what you do. It avoids having to Listen, Show Respect and Ask Why to yourself.

And here we go from one hyped up ICT development to another, hoping it will bring the solution or salvation we crave. What does it say about us if we constantly crave heroic acts, heroes and solutions? Do we feel we are not ok and need saving? What is the big example these people represent? Status, money, power? Being liked, followed and tweeted about? Is that what we aspire to? Is that it?

Companies such as Facebook and Google take the approach to the human as resource to a whole new level. Or perhaps more aptly put, depth. They use their customers as bait for advertisers so they can fill their pockets and have no qualms selling the information of their "customers" as a product. They sell the human resource to the highest bidder and see the resource as collateral damage to their money making scheme. In the twenty-first century, they digitally trade in people. Us & Them as in superior and inferior. The question we can ask ourselves is: is this what we want? Is this the game we want to play? Or do we dare to challenge ourselves and them, dare to reflect, do we dare to question ourselves and them, do we dare to listen to ourselves and act accordingly?

The combination of a voracious appetite for money making as a sole value to strive for, the hubristic idea of some kind of higher purpose to ICT and its insane pace of producer-pushed developments makes for a situation that reeks of the sorcerer's apprentice without the Walt Disney innocence.

Are leaders and executives ever challenged, questioned and held to account? When we read about another corporate fiasco or excess and wonder why this wasn't corrected internally it is worth having a closer look at the role of the non-executive director. The whole point of a non-executive director is, among other things, "to provide a creative contribution to the board by providing objective criticism." (The role of the non-executive Directors by the Institute of Directors.)

The 1992 Cadbury reports, which the above mentioned Institute of Directors cites, state non-executive directors "should bring an independent judgement to bear on issues of strategy, performance and resources including key appointments and standards of conduct."

There is no legal distinction between executives and non-executives and as a consequence the non-executives have the same legal duties, responsibilities and potential liabilities as their executive counterparts, although of course the distinction lies in the fact non-executive directors have no direct executive responsibilities, as in the day-to-day running of the company.

They are, however, just as responsible for the existing organizational culture and values within the company as the executive board members. In the Guidance note of UK Institute of the Administration of Chartered Secretaries and Administrators of January 2013 titled *Liability of non-executive directors: care, skill and diligence* point 6.3 states that prior to joining a board, prospective non-executive directors should:

> ... recognize that part of a non-executive director's role is to uphold high standard of integrity and probity, and to support the chairman and executive directors in instilling the appropriate culture, values and behaviours in the boardroom and beyond. During the discussions held prior to being offered a directorship, new non-executive directors should use the opportunity to ask questions about, and make judgement on, the culture, values and behaviours associated with the board.

The CIO is an executive and has the day-to-day responsibility regarding information streams and their security and privacy, apart from articulating the ICT strategy and policy. CIOs have ICT knowledge, to a more or lesser degree, but what about the non-executive directors? If they must provide objective criticism we can understand the necessity that they have enough knowledge in breadth and depth to be able to assess potential risks, especially considering the strong dependence of businesses on ICT. On C-level we may expect a healthy critical and discerning mind in relation to ICT and not singing hallelujah too fast when a new product is launched and presented as the next best thing. How much do non-executive directors know about ICT and the (ethical) implications? Is there objective criticism? And what is it focused on?

If leading by example is the name of the game, what example are executives and non-executives giving? Leading is one thing; perhaps the "led" don't want to be led in this manner. Is the example the executives and non-executives "lead" with, worthy of leadership?

DOING THE RIGHT THING, RIGHT, THE FIRST TIME

The title of this section has evolved as I was writing this book. Originally it was called "Do it right the first time." My focus was on adequate planning, decent software design, thorough testing, successful implementation and a customer service that doesn't imply ad infinitum adjustments and error removal … do it right the first time.

It was however, not only about doing *it* right, but doing *the right thing*, right. So here we are with an extended title which covers, for me at least, all the relevant elements. I was triggered directly by Dr. Klamer's book (2016) titled "Doing the right thing, a value based economy," so all credit goes to him for inspiring this last modification.

Let's go back to the definition of standard economics we saw before: standard economics is the science that studies the allocation of scarce resources, or the science of rational choice. It seems to be about survival (of the fittest?), overcoming hardship and the way to do that is to strive for more growth, income and profit. As we saw earlier in this chapter, the striving for continuous growth, income and profit is achieved, managed and sustained with the help of the double entry quantified registration representing their value in money.

It has led organizations, countries and individuals to value money, depicted on the "correct" side of either the balance sheet, the income statement, the cash-flow statement or the statement of retained earnings, as the goal to strive for through production, distribution and consumption of goods. Our relationships as organizations with our customers, suppliers and other stakeholders have been and are defined and influenced by this way of thinking and view of the (business) world. We have seen and continue seeing the consequences.

Money is an instrument, a means to achieve something we value. But the instrument has become the goal itself: the pursuit of profit and money has become our ultimate goal. The more money, the better, it seems. This way of thinking takes the focus away from the values which ultimately do fulfill us, such as honesty, integrity, probity. We have phased the values, for which we use the means of money, out of the equation. Values, such as prudence, courage and justice are sidelined.

What values are we talking about? An example: as an individual and as a wife or husband, mother or father of a family she or he will want to make money to pay a rent or a mortgage, buy food to feed the family, buy clothes, pay for education for his or her children to give them a chance to stand on their own two feet when they grow up and use the money to enjoy music, exhibitions, sports etc. We are happy when we are in good health, when our family is as well and when we can enjoy time together and with others: all these are the ends we pursue. We strive for the things—tangible and not tangible—we consider worthwhile. Money enables a lot of these things. This is just an example and it will be different for people. Whether you are in company or alone, we all desire happiness and harmony in relations.

When we apply this example to a bigger context, that of an organization, what are the things, the goods, the values we strive for? What are the company's ideals? The mission statement should answer those questions.

When you ask founders of companies such as Microsoft, Apple, Mars, Dell, Boeing or Toyota why they started the company, what drove them, what they considered important, they never answer with: I did it to make a lot of money. It makes for interesting reading what the core values are of ICT companies.

Facebook's mission is: "Give people the power to build community and bring the world closer together." And in a 2012 letter to potential investors the CEO outlines the five core values as Focus on Impact, Move Fast, Be Bold, Be Open and Build Social Value. About Being Open he says: "We believe that a more open world is a better world because people with more information can make better decisions and have a greater impact. That goes for running our company as well. We work hard to make sure everyone at Facebook has access to as much information as possible about every part of the company so they can make the best decisions and have the greatest impact." He fails to mention access applies to outsiders as well to be able to use people's private information "so they can make the best decisions and have the greatest impact." Indeed.

As for Build Social Value: "Facebook exists to make the world more open and connected, and not just to build a company. We expect everyone at Facebook to focus every day on how to build real value for the world in everything they do." Yes, it is clear Facebook's real "values" are considerably different from their "users." Once again we see that writing something down and acting upon those values can be two very different things. Especially when a lot of money is involved.

From a standard economics perspective value equates price. ICT companies are no different than any other organization which has adopted planned obsolescence as a strategy and considers money the end and not the means to achieve their (so called) values.

The vicious circle we are in is: producers manufacture products and services with a short replacement cycle so that the consumer buys continuously. The economy is focused on stimulating the user to consume without end but the consumer, to be able to consume, needs money, so the desire for money (the means) has been upgraded to the ultimate desired end. When the consumer has money and has been made to believe consuming is what makes him happy, as a consumer you buy and buy. Consumers cater to the desires of producers and go along with it. The producers and consumers have one thing in common though: their ultimate value is money. ICT companies are very much part of this dynamic and the result is what I define as the production of ICT fast food.

As we have seen before, the short replacement cycle doesn't stimulate manufacturing products or delivering services which are meant to last very long. They are meant for fast and instant consumption and to satisfy the producer's planned desire, money, and the consumer's influenced desire, the instant fix. Consequently, there is no rush nor authentic intention to manufacture or deliver a product or service which endures. The rate with which new frameworks, methodologies and models are introduced is to keep pace with this continuous churning out of ICT gadget burgers. A diet of fast food is not exactly nutritional and certainly not advisable to be consumed as the standard staple if health is a value we cherish.

We don't seem to care about doing the right thing, doing it right and doing it right the first time. The irony of this way of thinking is that if we did, it would cost us all less in the long run, that is, if our values and ideals are the end and not sec the money as the ultimate goal. Because by making money the end goal, we create a lot of waste. Products and services have to be replaced and the old discarded in an ever accelerated run. The popularity of AI and robots is no surprise: they enable producers to go faster and faster; people, being defective machines, make producers go slower and slower. We have made the twenty-first century the age of sloppiness, carelessness and laziness in how we do business, how we communicate, in our manners, in our thinking and in our morals and ethics.

Organizations are not external to society, to the environment or the market they operate in. They are part of the community, they are influenced *by* it and they influence *it* with the values they uphold and strive for. They are part of a complex system. With their choice of values and ideals they make a statement about how they wish to influence the system they are part of and how they wish to impact society.

So what effects do you wish to have on your own employees, on your customers, your suppliers, on the environment and society as a whole? Looking at ever increasing dependency of societies on ICT, and the colossal impact ICT has on communities, do ICT companies consider the general interest? Do they consider societies' values and ideals? The general organizational interests are imbedded within the grander system, the public general interest. As ICT organizations, do you view life in a linear way, do you go from A to B, or are you part of a greater system and do you realize there are multiple effects when you act, or do not act, in a certain way? Do you care?

What about other industries when we look at doing the right thing, right, the first time? No worries, they fine-tune with agility as they go along … We built your house without forethought and a plan so the water drips down our wall? Ah, we'll find some solution. We designed a bridge with cracks. Ah, we'll slap on some concrete or plaster and all is fine. We design a car with faulty brakes? Ah, better luck next time. We didn't protect your information enough and it's out there being used by criminals? Ah, too bad, live with it. Oh, nobody noticed the breaks, the cracks, the leaks, the faults? That's good, we got away with it!

Is it ok to consciously manufacture shoddy products and let consumers pay for those because you are savvy in marketing? Is it ok to look the other way knowingly because a lot of money can be made?

Uncomfortable questions perhaps, but organizations do not operate in isolation from society and separate from the people who work there and who buy their products and/or services. If all the above questions are answered with an affirmative, what does that make you? What do you stand for? What kind of a dynamic and what kind of a (business) world have we created? We have sacrificed our ideals and values. We are continuously opting out of them. More on this moral split in the next section.

Capitalism as we know it today and how it is being enacted with the double entry view of the world has led to double standards. We must revise how we define capitalism, which values we consider important and how we wish to shape our capitalism in this modern age. As Dr. Klamer expresses and explains in his book, a more value-based economy and value-based worldview is called for.

When organizations go off track and do not act in accordance with their ideals and values, when they are not aligned with the general interest, stakeholders become restless, uncomfortable and unhappy because some see what the impact is, but we all feel it, whether we are conscious of it or not. People try to change the dynamic, address the issue, leave, are "let go" or when matters have a considerable negative impact on the general interest, blow the whistle.

For a lot of companies money *is* considered the means to an end. For them money is the instrument to achieve the ultimate goal: power. Money and power go hand in hand. The questions which arise then are: power to use for what? To do what? Why?

How do ICT service providers fit into that context? If we look at the big tech companies such as Facebook, Google, Apple, etc., apart from societies' dependence, what do they want to use their power for? How are they wielding their power? Are they interested in doing the right thing? For the common good? What are their values, in deeds, not just in words? What are they up to and for what reason? Who do they associate with? Why? The ICT fast food they are producing and a society gorging on it leads to gasses and contorted digestive functions with social media platforms as the outlets for the generated mental diarrhea.

Our approach to doing business, to life for many, has been and still is defined by the duality based economic model that is all pervasive in our society. Is this way of doing business serving a purpose, is it for the benefit of all or is it to serve but a few, no matter the cost to the business environment, culture, the environment in a broader sense, to the welfare and happiness of people etc. We are stuck in a thinking and acting habit that is going against us, such as an addiction. We know it isn't good but we keep on feeding that habit. There is a very informative and useful book on understanding how our habits form and how to change them by Charles Duhigg, *The Power of Habit* (2012). We are addicted. Addicted to speed, fast money making, money making per se, power. The raison d'être of companies (and governments) is this? The common good of all who have a role within the company … or the few? Changing habits is changing attitude. Chapter 4, The Way Forward gives some suggestions where to start to achieve the desired changes.

What would happen if we made the conscious choice to let go of this approach? To not play the game according to the double entry "rules," but to create new ways of interacting, healthier ones? And if we release our perception of reality based on duality? On the this and that, us and them, superior and inferior? What if we embraced value based economics, value based business decisions, value based interactions, value being created because you combine elements, share them and create something new that benefits all parties and which permits you to look in the mirror in the morning with a clear conscience?

What we need is a bit of practical wisdom. Dr. Klamer writes about practical wisdom extensively and I will quote his definition. "Acting upon our values in pursuit of some good or another, and applying all available knowledge in doing so, is called phronesis, a term the Greek philosopher Aristotle uses and which means practical wisdom. Aristotle considers phronesis a cardinal virtue, that is, a virtue that is crucial for all valuations, for all actions. *A virtue is a value that we attribute to actions.*"

Another clarification of what phronesis means is given by Gonzalo Bustamente who "wrote a thesis on the subject. He explains that it calls for thoughtfulness, awareness of the goods to strive for and the relevant values, and a clear understanding on what people want and need, proven practices and strategies (Bustamante Kuschel, 2012)." More on phronesis in Chapter 4, The Way Forward.

I make a case for reflection, for slowing down, for taking time to think, to feel, to mull things over, to take time to make sure something is thought through, designed well, to build with intelligence, to make sure it works and stands the test of time. This means doing things with ethics, not because there is a written code of ethics (which is disregarded with ease) but with internal ethics. You act with a conscience, with principles; you realize you are part of society, you help shape it and therefore have a responsibility. You act according to the general interest as much as your own. You act with phronesis, with honesty towards your customers, your employees, your stake (share) holders and last but not last, yourself.

MORAL SPLIT

The emphasis on the linear and narrow duality approach and planned obsolescence interpretation of professional life leads to moral dilemmas. Professionals have studied at university and schools where they learned to cherish knowledge and do things well; for them to be forced to work in a planned obsolescence and/or poorly designed product/service environment where you are required to stay mum creates stress and unhappiness, with all related consequences.

Employees on operational level don't have much choice. They have to follow orders and cannot protest too much because it will have consequences for their career development. Their bosses on tactical level are always in a squeeze. Wedged between strategic and operational level they have the challenge to translate the top strategic policies down to operational level and reporting operational information bottom up to their bosses. They don't have much maneuvering space. As for strategic level; they tend to live according to their own VIP rules. They are the ones who articulate the planned obsolescence of quality and desirability strategies and sanction the related actions.

As discussed before, the organizational culture is defined and enacted by the attitude and behavior of C-suite level leaders and managers. So when we want to understand where we stand morally and ethically within ICT organizations, with colleagues and employees, and without, in our relationships with our customers and suppliers and in extension with society, we have to start with them.

When we go back to the Guidance note of the UK Institute of the Administration of Chartered Secretaries and Administrators of January 2013 titled *Liability of non-executive directors: care, skill and diligence* point 6.3 cited earlier on it states (my bold highlights):

> recognize that part of a non-executive director's role is **to uphold high standard of integrity and probity**, and to support the chairman and executive directors in instilling the **appropriate culture, values and behaviours in the boardroom and beyond**. During the discussions held prior to being offered a directorship, new non-executive directors should use the opportunity to ask questions about, and make judgement on, the culture, values and behaviours associated with the board.

Although this statement is about non-executives, it applies to the executives as well; they are directly responsible for the day to day operations in their organizations and have therefore a very direct impact. To start with, are high standards of integrity and probity upheld within the organization? Are the leaders and managers the example of integrity and probity? Does the organizational culture, its values and the behavior of those leaders and managers reflect those high standards? Do the leaders and managers instill the values and behaviors and are those visible and palpable in the organizational culture?

Related to the previous section, which values and ideals do we uphold at strategic level and translate down to tactical an operational level? The specific day to day running of a business with its various necessary skills and expertise can be delegated to the people who have those necessary skills and expertise. But integrity, honesty, authenticity, probity and other (moral) values cannot be delegated. Real leadership is having the moral authority to lead. Real leaders embody the values.

To avoid misunderstandings I will use the description and cite from Jerald Greenberg and Robert A. Baron's *Behavior in Organizations* (2004) on the relationship and difference between moral values and ethics: "Moral values (morals) are people's fundamental beliefs regarding what is right or wrong, good or bad. Ethics are standards of conduct that guide people's decisions and behavior (e.g. not stealing from others) and business ethics refer to the behavior in morally appropriate ways in organizations." Ethics is about conduct.

So where does the moral split come from that I use as title of this section? It comes from not practicing what leaders preach, from not translating the values integrity, honesty, authenticity, probity to tactical level and then not enabling managers on tactical level to translate those yet again to operational level. When there is a disconnect between words and deeds and to what is said and done on strategic, tactical and operational level, the balance is gone and people on those three levels—mostly tactical and operational—end up in dire straits and as a result the organization as a whole starts sliding down a slippery slope.

As service providers, how can we look the customer in the eye and say customer satisfaction is on the top of our list if the products and services we provide are designed and built with the purpose of breaking down? When we create products which have to be replaced because they cease to function properly? When we are focused on an ever shortening of the replacement cycle?

Can leaders and managers on strategic level look their employees in the eye and not blink when they vocalize their truths and values? The managers and leaders on tactical level have to make those words happen in the rest of the organization. And on operational level they will have plenty of questions and desire for clarification since they are the ones who see and feel it the most when words are different from actions. But they are the ones who have to put out the fires, save the day and make things happen. In Chapter 1 we saw what happens when communication and information flows don't flow. People on operational level suffer the most because they have nowhere to go, especially when the organizational culture is one of fear, as we shall see more in detail in the next chapter.

People on operational level are faced with considerable difficulties when the inconsistencies stare them in the face and when they have to make decisions. The big dilemma is how far you go appeasing your manager and acting for the (monetary) benefit of your organization but knowing it is not right and knowing you are sidelining your customer. We have read and still read plenty of examples from the financial world about the morally unsavory practices but also the ICT world is in the news often enough regarding this topic. From a personal experience, I was once asked on two different occasions by two managers, one on the highest level, to sign a blank in course assessment document to let an important customer, who had not passed it, get the result he and the company I worked for wanted. I refused (and so did my colleague with whom I assessed the students) and have certainly been made to feel it. The reason for not changing these morally hollow ways of being is always money and power. And the prevailing attitude and mindset is that as long as no one knows and you can get away with it, it is ok.

When we are children we learn about morals and ethics. We are taught to show respect, not to lie, not to steal, to be honest and kind, to do our homework, to behave. We are taught to throw waste in the wastepaper basket, to not make a mess and to clean up. We don't learn at school to cut corners; the teachers don't let us. We don't learn to cut corners on moral and ethical issues. We are corrected by our teachers, peers and at home. So what happens later on? Why do we cut corners when we work? Why is that acceptable? Is it acceptable because you get away with it? Has the cutting corners attitude and behavior infected us to such a degree we don't question it anymore? Is the mutation of the organizational system in such an advanced stage we are (have become) the (mutated) children of our own questionable creation?

So once again: Is it morally acceptable to ask your employees to design and do things that you know are faulty, that have errors, that don't benefit the customer? Is it morally acceptable to design and make products that break down or become obsolete *on purpose* with the goal of forcing people to fork out more money for the next version or model? Is it morally acceptable to treat customers like this and accept their money by fostering a dependency with the planned obsolescence of desirability strategy? Is it morally acceptable to market a product which you know is crappy? What kind of business does that remind us of, creating addictive behavior? And then present yourself as the savior for a better world where everything is "smarter"?

The answer is: no, it is not morally acceptable. We have created and maintain an immoral system. The system we have created is based on double standards, the people who are consciously sustaining this system have chosen to opt out of values and ideals. Planned obsolescence of quality and desirability are wrong in essence and structurally rotten. An economy and business strategies based on consumers servicing producers by being forced and coerced into spending continuously and in ever shorter replacement cycles is unethical, unhealthy and has put us in the downward spiral of destruction of happiness, wellbeing and (moral) health: on a personal, organizational and planetary level.

ICT service providers and other types of IT organizations have a very crucial and important responsibility because they manage the information (flow) of their customers. Privacy and security of the customer's data is inherently part of their core business. Unfortunately, this is the area where they are too often found most wanting. Massive data collection, personal data being sold for petty financial gain (and power) and severe lapses in protection of data is happening as I write. It is unethical and even illegal. It is also dangerous. The collaboration between ICT and governmental institutions makes for tantalizing temptations for those in power to (ab)use the data, to link it, to change it to serve their goals. An example from my own country, The Netherlands, shows how far this collaboration has gone.

The paper-based tickets to travel by train, tram, bus and metro were replaced by the OV-chipkaart (short for *openbaar vervoer chipkaart*, meaning *public transport chipcard*) covering a time span from 2005 to 2014. It is a contactless smart card which you top up with credit and use to pay for your journey. It can function as a stored-value card which you use to travel on with pre-loaded credit or you can store "travel products" on it such as day passes, seasonal tickets or single and return rail tickets. The traveler must check in at the beginning of his journey and check out at the end by passing the card over an OV-chip card reader.

I will not go into all the details of the controversy surrounding this card but limit myself to pointing out that by using this system information on where you begin your journey, where you finish it, how long it took you and how frequent you travel that particular route is known to the five large public transport operators. You are fined when you do not check out. Your travel data is collected and so is your personal data. Linking those two pools of information permits the public travel operators and the card operator to track passengers and build an image of an individual's travel behavior. Violations of Dutch privacy legislation in 2007 showed these two types of information were stored together and unlawful monitoring of travelers' behavior was at risk and in 2012 personal data was used for marketing purposes. Action was taken and corrective measures taken. All we can do now is keep our fingers crossed.

Another example is when you park your car and buy a ticket at the parking meter. Parking meters throughout the country are all becoming digital so instead of buying the ticket and putting the ticket in your car where it is visible, you have to enter your license plate number, the time and you are done. This is the case in Amsterdam. Scan cars and scan scooters collect your information, which is stored in a national database which currently 68 municipalities are linked to. There was and is a lot of protest by drivers about having to share their license plate number information just because they are parking somewhere. It means you can be tracked and monitored. In 2016 The Supreme Court ruled you are not in the obligation to share your license plate number. Parking meters in Amsterdam still haven't changed.

Companies and governments expect people to trust them not to do anything improper with their data. To be able to trust someone or trust an entity the behavior and actions of that person have to warrant the trust. The behavior and actions of (ICT) companies and governmental institutions have shown us again and again that the trust is mostly not warranted. They don't want to or do not have the proper security measures in place to be able to guarantee no shady business is going on with your information.

Just as the flipped dynamic of the planned obsolescence attitude and actions where customers cater to the demands of producers, in this case the tables have also been turned in the sense that employees and citizens are forced to be constantly on the alert and actually have to be highly suspicious because multiple cases have shown that their privacy and security are breached on a large scale. Ethical rhetoric and ethical actions show a considerable divide.

Bernard Burnes states in *Managing Change* (2004) in the section about Business ethics: "According to Teather (2002), the hyping or 'ramping' of shares was central to the operation of Wall Street's financial institutions and not just limited to a few rogue analysts. In May 2003, in an attempt to draw a line under the crimes of the boom years, leading Wall Street financial institutions agreed to pay fines totaling $ 1.4 billion (Tran, 2003). Nevertheless, corporate greed was not limited to Wall Street, and much of it was quite legal." 2008 happened and in 2018 we are back to the same practices. A few financial institutions went bankrupt and many were bailed out by governments.

The sentence about the hyping and ramping up of shares can be applied to the ICT sector: … the hyping and ramping up of ICT products and services is central to the operation of Silicon Valley and beyond and not just limited to a few rogue companies. It is their business strategy.

As for the statement: "Nevertheless, corporate greed was not limited to Wall Street, and much of it was quite legal"; we can say the same thing regarding the ICT sector. Both sectors have adopted and work according to the double entry and planned obsolescence strategy where money and power are the coveted end. In 2018 the attitude and behavior haven't changed, the rhetoric has, and now we have governance and ethics codes, right?

We have even gone so far down the slippery slope we have reached the point where malpractice and unethical behavior is rewarded. Top level management who have failed miserably but leave the company with humongous pay outs occur regularly. They are rewarded for failure and just as often awarded for unethical behaviour. Not only in regards to their customers but also towards their own employees. The paying of enormous amounts of money despite very serious unethical behavior, e.g., as Google has done with the sexual harassment cases, shows the (un) ethical standards are alive and kicking. The term that comes to mind is hush money.

In Burnes' words: "As the discussion of sustainability, diversity and ethics shows, however, globalization also raises crucial questions about the role and impact of organizations on and in a global society. These questions go beyond the traditional business concerns such as profit and loss, value for money or market share; they are concerned with fundamental issues of the role of organizations in sustaining life on Earth, respect for human diversity and dignity, and the ethical rules by which we live … Governments, international bodies and individual organizations have responded by adopting policies that supposedly promote responsible and ethical behavior … Nevertheless, the gap between ethical rhetoric and the reality of unethical behavior seems to be getting wider rather than narrower. The real challenge for organizations is to change managerial behavior so that business ethics become business practices. Policies, skills and good intentions are clearly not enough." The lack of basic psychological insight and moral and ethical development with the associated missing compass is evident.

Are all ICT companies and service providers as I described above? No, there will be ethically sound organizations whose deeds and actions are in sync and not to worry about. Unfortunately they are becoming scarcer since the new normal is the opposite and has been so already for a long time. It is becoming increasingly difficult for sound ICT companies to remain as such since they operate in a system which has other "values" at its foundation.

We have to be careful when we blame the system when things are murky. When we point our finger to the "system" it is a way to create distance between the unethical way of working and our own contribution to that way of working. A "system" in itself, as a separate entity, doesn't exist, nor does "the market" or "capitalism" or "the organizational culture." They are all created and operate as such because people have created them that way and maintain them functioning in that manner. People are their creators and enablers; people define the mechanism, the dynamic, the way of working of the "system," "the market," "capitalism" or "organizational culture." If you want to change any of those systems, you will have to change the attitudes and behavior of people. That implies change in their moral values, in how they enact them. Change of morals, business ethics and a system such as double entry thinking and doing and planned obsolescence strategies can only change when people do, from the inside out.

As long as we don't address our inner development, our inner growth, our inner work, nothing will change. Because we will continue with our grand egos and convictions we are creating a better world with our products and services. The starting point is the individual. The values of a company are the extension of the values of a group of individuals. Management who define and articulate the strategies and ethics policies, in words and deeds, steer the company to do business in a particular way and impact their environment with their business interactions.

So actually, there is no out there and in here. Just as there is no out there and in here with an oil slick that extends and extends until everything is an oil stain and dark and stinky. Instead of an oil stain, we could extend authenticity, integrity, honesty, probity. Instead of oil, what about a transparent shower of rain which nourishes everybody? Every single day we make a choice. Oil burns and pollutes, water fosters growth.

The enemy is fear. We think it is hate; but, it is fear

Mahatma Gandhi

Fear is, I believe, a most effective tool in destroying the soul of an individual—and the soul of a people

Anwar Sadat

3

The Fear Factor

Dancing to the tune of the Pied Piper
Professionals versus zombies
Moral burn out and ethical obsolescence

DANCING TO THE TUNE OF THE PIED PIPER

In Chapter 1 we saw the sorry state of affairs regarding the relationship between service providers, customers and their suppliers. The dynamic created in the information and communication flows between these parties are not to be particularly enthusiastic about, resulting in customer dissatisfaction. We have also seen that the communication and information flows within the companies themselves are murky or stagnant with all related undesired implications.

In Chapter 2 we delved into the cause of these troubled relations. We have adopted a duality oriented approach to (business) life and created business strategies based on a planned obsolescence premise. The result is we have trapped ourselves, willingly and unwillingly, into a continuous need and desire for buying, spending and therefore making money to maintain the system. The system we created is like a monster which needs to be continuously fed to keep it satisfied. This Planned Obsolescence system creates a lot of waste, for which we are paying the price on a global scale.

Presently we are living in a flipped reality where consumers must cater to the demands and wishes of the producer and to sustain this upside down profitable strategy for producers, the consumers must be kept running in the hamster wheel of the ever shorter replacement cycle. Apart from the consumers, the producers must, consciously and unconsciously, want and believe this upside down system as being the way you do things, the only way of doing them and feeling good about it to dampen any inner feeling of doubt or expression of conscience. A perfect tool to discourage any discontent or potential rebellion is fear.

Let's start with the consumers, aka the customer. The planned obsolescence of desirability ties into the fear factor seamlessly. The reason people buy the product when put on the market by the producer is because if you don't, you are not part of the club, the lucky few. You score even higher points when you are one of the first 100 to have bought the new phone, tablet or super-duper watch. Or related to the service provider world: if you are not adopting AI, putting everything in the cloud or not implementing that new methodology or best practice, your will miss the boat to a bright future.

These are fears. Fears of not being perceived as modern, up to date, fear to miss something, fear to be considered less desirable or likeable, fear not to be number one. Fear not be considered part of the "group" and be seen as a loser. Planned obsolescence of desirability feeds off the fear of rejection and exclusion and has insecurity and/or an inferior complex at its core. People are no different from animals in the sense they want to be part of the herd—in people's case, the tribe—and feel protected and appreciated by it. That is a normal desire but we all know the time comes for a questioning of or separation from the tribe, either physically, mentally and/or emotionally, to choose and make your own destiny. To be true to yourself and take charge of your own life. You can choose to stay, but then you are required to conform. This is, after all, why we can live together in harmony because we abide by the laws. However, the tribe can have questionable intentions or intentions that don't tally with yours and can act with mounting ferocity to the outsider, the non-conformer, as so well depicted in William Golding's 1954 book *Lord of the Flies*. The modern day variation to the theme is not restricted to an island anymore, but has spread to the mainland as well and is rapidly played out with the use of ICT and social media on a global level.

Consumers and customers are encouraged to conform. We have reached the point where they gladly do so because the alternative is too confrontational. The alternative would be to look closely at yourself and ask the questions: *why* am I afraid? *What* am I afraid of? Are the "consequences" of non-conformity to the Planned obsolescence inspired tribe scaring me? What does it say about me, if I am? What values do I hold dear and (would like to) act upon?

The fears mentioned before position the power and the definition of who you are, outside of you, in the hands of others. Others define who you are, what you should look like, what you should do and when and what you should buy. Or else … They present it however, as if *you* desire it. How well do you know yourself? What is your driving force? The point is: do *I* define who *I* am and how *I* act or does an outside party push my buttons and program my reactions?

And what about fear on the producers' side? When we use the term fear perhaps the first thing that comes to mind is the culture of fear where there is a tyrannical boss who shouts, puts you down, disrespects you etc. These behaviors are quite obvious and clear fear inspiring bully tactics and to be seen as an expression on the far end of the pendulum. What I would like to address here is the more subtle culture of fear which is present in our own minds and ingrained within organizational cultures and dynamics. We are often not aware of its presence but it does define our attitude and behavior.

In the previous chapter we saw an organization is a system and the system has a self-regulating way of correcting and keeping in check the elements which are perceived as not conforming. Comparable to the auto immune system of the body. Elements perceived as a danger or threat to the health of the system are attacked, eliminated or isolated. Within organizations the same happens. An organizational culture becomes a self-regulating system once the way of thinking and doing are instilled and it becomes so much part of us we don't question it anymore, but just act a certain way, because that is "how we do things here."

The types of fear we see in organizations and the ones already mentioned for the consumers are e.g. the fear of making mistakes, fear of failure, fear of not being popular and even the fear of success. The underlying fears are the more personal ones: fear to lose your job, to not be able to pay the rent, pay school fees and fear not to be able to put food on the table.

Due to the fact we have elevated the making and spending of money as our highest value and the ultimate goal to strive for, the activities which permit us to obtain the much desired money must be worked hard for and protected. Any threat and danger must be contained and risks managed and avoided. Fear, very useful to keep us alert and alive, has now taken over as one of the main emotions driving human behavior. Consequently, it is used by people and organizations with their particular interests to achieve their goals.

How many of us can recall situations where we had serious doubts about a chosen path, decision or action at our workplace and we decided not to say anything? Do we remember why we chose not to speak up? The fear of discomfort, of rocking the boat, of questioning … the hassle, and danger of it leads to conforming; it is the easy way out. It is easier to turn our head, to pretend we didn't see, we didn't hear, we didn't feel than look the uncomfortable situation and/or person in the eye and address it. The discomfort is unpleasant, awkward and tense situations will occur. That is exactly what people who do unethical things count on; that you don't dare to address it and so that self-censorship takes place.

Fear "freezes" people, paralyses them. The old survival mode kicks in. You keep a low profile and hope the danger will disappear. In the animal world creatures play dead as a survival technique. Employees play "dead" too; the corporate dead who keep a low profile to survive and eventually drift as dead wood to the top. Don't protest too much, don't disagree, don't rock the boat. That's how fear works. And for those in the decision-making positions who benefit from little questioning and critical observation this is very useful. They take advantage of the situation to proceed on a path they have set out and consider best. This is perpetuated consciously (management by fear) and unconsciously due to lack of (self-) awareness regarding this dynamic. It is the reason fear, a negative awe, is a strategy in warfare. Used to dominate and to paralyze the adversary and thus have the upper hand. In organizations those are the loudmouths in every meeting; a bit of fear inspiring organizational bullying. With the Planned Obsolescence dynamic to (business) life and the fact we all go along with it, we see a case of group think in extremis on corporate, national and even global level.

However, where *you* are in the organizational hierarchy will have a big influence on your decision. The ease with which you can be laid off, fired or "let go" feeds off fear and maintains a culture where employees will conform and accept behavior which otherwise they wouldn't or would question more openly. Specifically employees on operational level, on the lowest rung of the corporate ladder, are in the most difficult position and do not have much choice. As we have seen previously, the tone for the organizational culture is set on strategic level and implemented down from there to tactical and operational level. And although professionals may not be in the position to protest due to the potential dire consequences they do notice and take note. They will eventually, as they choose to climb up the corporate ladder, assimilate the culture and participate actively or passively or perhaps they will leave either willingly or unwillingly or blow the whistle. Healthy checks and balances are phased out with fear for the consequences of speaking up.

Psychoanalyst and Professor of leadership development and organizational change at INSEAD, Dr. Manfred Kets de Vries, in his book *The Leader on the Couch* (2006) states: "The repetition of phenomena ... in a given workplace suggests the existence of shared scripts in the inner theater of the key powerholders. Organizations tend to reflect the personalities of their leaders [19 and 20], because leaders externalize and act out their inner theater on the public stage of the organization. Their inner dramas develop into corporate cultures, structures, and specific patterns of decision-making. Because leaders 'institutionalize' the themes of their inner theater, their influence may continue long after they themselves have gone, determining how the next generation in power runs things."

He continues with: "Exemplary leaders help their companies become highly effective organizations, while dysfunctional leaders contribute to a dysfunctional organizational culture and organizational 'neurosis'. He identifies five types of neurotic organizations, summarized via archetypical methodology as the dramatic/cyclothymic organization, the suspicious organization, the compulsive organization, the detached organization and the depressive organization. The aspects of these five organizations tend to perform in a hybrid form.

A dramatic/cyclothymic is characterized by senior management with "an intense drive to receive positive attention from outsiders. They like to impress others ..., favor superficiality in all things, demonstrate great swings of emotion, often act on the basis of hunches and gut feelings, and tend to react (or overreact) to minor events." The example he gives is Richard Branson's Virgin Group, successful and wanting to get attention and impress important people.

Within suspicious organizations there is "a general atmosphere of distrust and paranoia (especially among the leadership), hypersensitivity to hidden meanings and motivations as well as to relationships and organizational issues, hyper-alertness for problems, and a constant, vigilant outlook for the "enemy.""" Robert Maxwell's former empire and J. Edgar Hoover's FBI are examples.

The third type of neurotic organization Kets de Vries describes is the compulsive one, which is "preoccupied with trivialities and characterized by a highly rigid and well-defined set of rules, along with elaborate information systems and ritualized, exhaustive evaluation procedures." He mentions IBM under the leadership of John Akers as having many characteristics of this kind of organization with its ritualistic inward-looking focus.

The detached organization has a "cold, unemotional atmosphere … non-involvement with others in and outside the organization is the norm. These organizations, indifferent to praise and criticism alike, are characterized by lack of excitement and enthusiasm. The empire of hermit leader Howard Hughes possessed many of these detached characteristics."

And the fifth neurotic organization is defined as depressive. "Inactivity, lack of confidence, extreme conservatism, and insularity are the chief features of depressive organizations. They have 'a profoundly low sense of pride … strong sense of indecision, an unwillingness to take risks, a focus on diminishing or outmoded markets, undeveloped sense of competition, and apathetic and inactive leadership. Many organizations who do work for governments are depressive organizations, or hybrids that blend depressive and compulsive traits." After the founders of Disney and Reader's Digest died, the respective organizations showed these depressive characteristics.

In summary, we are speaking about neurotic organizations. When we look at how the ICT organizations are operating and interacting with their customers and suppliers and more specifically, when we see these parties all interact within the duality based, double entry Planned Obsolescence dynamic and psychology, the economic capitalist system as we know it today and as we have created it, is a neurotic system, operating with a neurotic market dynamism. It is a hybrid combination of the above-mentioned types, take your pick. And since we are the creators of this system, what we are doing is enacting our neurosis on the public stage of the global world.

Within this neurotic context the highly coveted innovations will be either very difficult to achieve due to the organizational culture present or the innovations will be an expression of the neurotic culture and system. What are we creating and from which state of (un)health? Innovation is high on the agenda and deemed necessary, the only option according to many, for (ICT) business in the twenty-first century. According to multiple publications and surveys, such as the 2018 Deloitte CIO global survey, companies either adapt and adopt the digital innovations or are doomed. A quote from the Deloitte survey, by Sara Mathew, board member of the Campbell Soup Company is: "IT has to innovate or die. Technology is moving at warp speed while humans move in a more linear fashion, so innovation is key. And to innovate well, we have to think about business through a digital lens." In this quote, technology is seen as an autonomous driving force to which the slow, linear operating humans have to adapt … or die.

Whether we agree or disagree with this statement, innovation within a company requires the creative juices to be able to flow. Fear, worry or preoccupation with your position within the company, what you can and cannot say, doesn't enhance creativity. It is one of the reasons companies are so interested in startups for innovative products. Startups don't (yet) have the consolidated and fixed strategic, tactical and operational level structure with its own particular dynamic. So if innovation is considered to make or break companies, they should perhaps enhance an organizational structure and culture which fosters creativeness and innovation. Fear nor neurosis have any space there. Yes, innovation is necessary, but not so much of a technological order than of a psychological one. The manner in which we do business and the values we hold high need innovation.

There is a severe lack of psychological development and (self) awareness and this has translated into the organizational cultures with a fear culture and organizational neurosis as the result. Fear is an excellent tool to use to keep people in check—don't rock the boat, don't question—which enables the duality attitude and behavior and planned obsolescence strategies to be maintained and kept firmly in place.

The fear however is not only used consciously and deliberately; there is an unconscious terror to look critically at ourselves and at the impact we have on our direct environment and on the environment in a broader context. Self-reflection and asking yourself honest questions can be painful and very confrontational; to be avoided at all costs! So we keep ourselves busy all day running from meeting to meeting, on the phone, online, always available so we are never alone with ourselves. Because when you are alone, the questions and feelings which can make you uneasy crop up. And that means taking responsibility for them. Do we look ourselves in the eye?

The earphones to keep us in our bubble with the constant streaming of music is a very welcome distraction from the deeper inner voice and keeps it comfortably at bay. We like ICT gadgets and their disruptiveness so much because it helps us not to look within. ICT products, items and services provided and marketed, especially by the big tech companies, are to keep us busy, tired and online (meaning traceable): they are the Masters of Mass Distraction.

To sum it up: all the above mentioned fears come into being from the core fear, the fear of ourselves. Fear of our dark side. Fear of asking ourselves the difficult questions and whether we are happy with what we have created and what we continue creating. Once again, it is confrontational and would force us to question what our beliefs and true values are.

We project our own shadow onto the outside world, our dark side is given form outside of us, on the other. Us and Them. Of course, we, as service providers, we as customers, we as providers, are on the right side. The danger, the threat, the inappropriate being-ness and behavior comes from the other and certainly does not lurk within ourselves: the customer doesn't get it, doesn't get involved enough, doesn't pay enough. The service provider is always behind schedule, doesn't deliver what we asked for, doesn't give good support. The supplier is slow, doesn't respect deadlines, is horrible in communication, and so on. The blame game is played within organizations as well as between the various business parties involved.

Perhaps that is why we have embraced the idea that humans are like machines. It saves us from the uncomfortable responsibility for our thinking, feeling and actions. We are only a machine and respond to stimuli, our buttons are pressed, we can't help it. It happens to us. Perhaps the manner in which science has developed is a pendulum reaction to the era of the power of the church and of the mysteries of God. We went from one end to the other. First we were but subjects of an almighty God—as presented especially by the Catholic Church who had all the power—and could not decide our own fate for we would be punished severely if we did not conform to the church's law (that in their view represented God's will) and then we exchanged that for rational science, where we were "proven" machines and where ratio and the rational approach were the leading force. The human being has a very strong desire for control. Our one sided approach to human being-ness with only rationalized science has led to distancing ourselves from our own human beingness, from the messy part of emotions, feelings etc. which "overcome" us and for which we can take no responsibility. The machine view has permitted us to approach our inner workings as rational algorithms we tinker with, but for which we do not take responsibility, because they happen to us. The irony is that our limited rational algorithmic view of life has become the new God we bow to, not out of respect though, but out of fear, once again.

Actually, we have chosen for moral and ethical cowardice. The sloppy thinking, sloppy doing, sloppy products and services are a result of moral and ethical laziness. We prefer instant satisfaction, no matter the cost and consequently the embrace of planned obsolescence. We prefer the ill system we have created above changing it. Additionally, the lure of money and power prove an exceptionally strong motivator and has created a compelling interest to be protected at all costs.

So the most convenient thing to do is choose the path of least resistance. We opt out of critical self-examination. We opt out of critical examination and questioning of the premises on which we base our way of doing business and what the impact is on our own companies, our customers, our providers, our society and on our planet. Après moi, le deluge. We have projected our shadow into and unto the outside world and are letting the shadow drive us; we have given it the reins of our lives, shrug helplessly and passively follow the tune of the Pied Piper.

What is the vision of the future we are projecting unto and into the world? Which thinking and feeling patterns do we give shape with our actions? The actions and practices of an organization, initiated on strategic level, are translated down to tactical and operational level through the policies, procedures and (inter) actions and thus form the culture.

If organizations wish to change their practices and/or culture the only way to do so structurally is to change the way they think, for that will change how they (inter)act. Solely changing the practices and behavior, for example with an ethical code, without changing the underlying thought processes and patterns means "mistakes" will continue to be made and the so called improvements will not endure. The new methodologies, frameworks, models and best practices, some of them perfectly viable and useful, will not endure. A "new" way of working is introduced and after a few months everybody is back to their own, old habits and/or have found creative courses of action to circumvent the new "best" practice.

Technological developments don't "happen" to us. It is not unavoidable "progress." We create them because we choose to do so. We (collectively) create something we hold in our mind's eye. We think it and crystallize our thoughts into products and services. WE do it. There is no exterior force doing the creating or forcing us to create it. So, what *do* we hold in our mind's eye and crystallize? Do we think and create products and services we are afraid of—we create what we fear—or do we create products which have an added value and which create benefit for the common good? We attract, we woo; with our focused and roused energy we bring into this world our creations.

Our focused attention defines the goal we pursue and we attract and are attracted by the people, situations and interactions of our projected desire. That, however, also includes the projection of our negative thinking, fears, worries and neurosis. What you do not wish to happen is so strong that the focused energy on not wanting it to happen creates the exact reality you don't want. Call it the Law of Attraction or more specifically the term is used when something happens we don't want, the self-fulfilling prophecy. If we wish to have healthy interactions and a healthy business environment for the common good and based on ethical values then it would help to project that image into the world, attract and be attracted to those principles and put our focused energy and efforts into achieving it in practice.

If we consider customers or consumers as idiots or solely as money making machines, we will treat them as such and create products service providers can make money with; all the consumers have to do is consume, and fast please. You create the continuous self-fulfilling "improvement" loop of seeing customers as addicted users of your products and as products themselves to be exploited and discarded for your own aggrandizement.

We should reclaim our power to think independently, to create our own reality—using our own five non enhanced senses—based on uplifting, positive and constructive values for the common good instead of consuming the barrage of fear and neurotic inspired messages with the intention of steering and manipulating our thinking into creating the reality which some prefer out of self-interest. If we are smart ourselves we do not need so called smart devices to harvest data about us and maneuver us into a thinking-lane with a programmed destiny.

With the help of technology and digitizing the steering and manipulation has been given an enormous boost and has made it considerably easier. It speeds up the process and facilitates the intended planned obsolescence and ever shorter replacement cycle reality. We should claim and take back our power over our minds and thinking and not outsource it—willingly— to so called smart devices and seemingly smart companies and— unwillingly—let ourselves be forced to accept digitization-of-everything, chips (preferably inserted into our bodies) and robots. We are creating a world where humanized robots are being preferred over actual humans. Is that the reality we want to crystallize into being?

PROFESSIONALS VERSUS ZOMBIES

The multiple fears and specifically the fear of ourselves lead to conforming, accepting, not questioning and following the Pied Piper's tune passively over the edge of the cliff. But it also culminates into not being creative, innovative, etc., in a healthy way. But isn't innovation exactly what organizations want and need? Creativeness and innovative-ness, however, cannot flourish in environments where people are scared to express themselves or when they have values which don't conform to the organizational culture.

The Forbes Insights survey, *Delivering Value to today's digital enterprise* (2017) and other surveys as well, indicates that people are not prepared enough to face and handle the challenges of the modern age of digitization. Why would that be? Do employees get the mental and emotional space to prepare? Are they facilitated and supported in this endeavor by their superiors? Does the organizational culture enable being prepared? Do employees get the time to attend courses and classes to learn and digest the new knowledge? Does the CIO acquire this new knowledge himself so he can show them the way? Or does he just accept its existence as a given and sigh at the challenge?

A major issue—and it is becoming worse by the day—is the discrepancy between the ever *increasing* workload and the ever *decreasing* amount of resources—people—who have to do the work. This situation leads to pressured, tired and overworked employees and employers. Work is giving energy, but also receiving it! If you go home exhausted and drained, what is the point? You can work hard but go home energized because you received energy back from people, because you were creative, productive, had harmonious and fun interactions, acquired new knowledge and perhaps learned something about yourself.

Fear leads to putting energy into worry, preoccupation, feelings of powerlessness and stress. It takes the energy away from more positive and productive thought processes and activities which would benefit the organization much more. Remove the stress and constant pressure on employees and they will be more relaxed, happier and as a result more productive. What we see however is a constant doing more with less people. We also see managers putting extra pressure on their already stressed employees because they don't manage their affairs in an effective and efficient manner and because they are victim of the same self-inflicted dynamic. It is very common to see managers asking or demanding their employees to take on more work when their agenda is already full and not indicating which activity they should suspend to meet the urgent request. They pile it on and subsequently blame the employee if mistakes are made. Work extra, what's the problem? Employees are overloaded. Something will have to give.

Employees are not the only ones suffering from pressure and stress. The employers themselves, up to the highest level, are under enormous pressure, not only due to the fact they are ultimately responsible and accountable but because they are victim of the same neurotic system and dynamic we have created. However, admitting on C-suite level you are reaching your breaking point is still a taboo and perceived as not professional and not becoming of a strong leader.

The comment often made in those circumstances is: "If you can't take the heat, clear out." On boardroom level, admitting things are becoming too much and that you cannot continue working 12 hours a day is a taboo subject: you will be labeled a loser. Managers who have fallen severely ill, have suffered a serious burnout or worse, have committed suicide, is a sad reality and is an indication we have created a toxic work environment and dynamic.

In the book by Manfred Kets de Vries et al.: *Coach and Couch: The Psychology of Making Better Leaders* (2nd edition 2016), a whole chapter is dedicated to executive stress. Related to the taboo aspect in Chapter 13 "*Executive Stress— Taboo or Opportunity for Change*" by Caroline Rook, Thomas Hellwig, and Elizabeth Florent-Treacy we read:

> Tackling executive stress poses challenges, as it seems to be both normalized and taboo. For some it seems routine to be under constant pressure, to sleep for only four hours a night, and to work at weekends (normalization). Furthermore, senior executives might want to appear strong in the eyes of staff and shareholders, and will not admit to signs of weakness or reduced performance (taboo). A "stiff upper lip" or "soldiering on" is still the norm in many organizational cultures. However, the normalization and taboo of executive stress can lead to a subjective experience of stress that is in fact dysfunctional and will eventually lead to burnout as the executive denies experiencing strain and fails to build resilience.

How are important decisions going to be made by leaders if they don't get enough sleep, hardly relax, are under constant strain to comply with deadlines, under pressure to always grow, to always make more money because that is what shareholder value apparently is solely about? What is the quality of the thinking process and of reflection on important matters? Where is the time, the quiet and the solitude to weigh and ponder and to be able to wander within and listen to your inner voice? To emphasize the serious issue of stress, the impact it has and the behavior it can encourage we continue with:

> The increasing costs of stress through sick leave and loss of employees have been widely reported. However, executive health has a particular impact on the performance of the organization. Prolonged work pressure leads to fatigue and burnout, which in turn result in absence that impacts on the performance of the organization. Pressure also affects the confidence of staff in their leader and the confidence of investors, while stress has an influence on leadership decisions. Extensive work demands lead to the increased use of heuristics to make decisions or imitation of the strategic actions of other organizations. Leaders under pressure also tend to delegate more work to subordinates and, if the pressure increases, may resort to bullying and threatening in order to meet the requirement for faster or better performance.

CIOs are now held responsible and looked at to define the ICT strategy and make it work within the company. ICT in 2019, however, is a responsibility of all C-suite level executives and of all managers on the tactical and operational levels of the organization. The CIO is the ICT expert, who should have the overview and clear understanding of the business and ICT aspects important for the company, but this does not exempt the other C-suite leaders from the responsibility of being proactive about acquiring knowledge and understanding ICT. The *combination* of the skills and expertise of the top executives makes a team strong and capable to lead the business into a future which is strongly defined by ICT, but which is not the sole critical success factor.

A trend which has taken root in many companies is what is coined as empowerment. Empowerment is giving employees the responsibility and authority to make decisions. It is the delegation of authority to the lower levels of the organization. Jerald Greenberg and Robert A. Baron identify three main facets of empowerment in their book *Behavior in Organizations* which involve:

- *Information sharing*: Providing potentially sensitive information on costs, productivity, quality, and financial performance to employees throughout the organization.

- *Autonomy through Boundaries*: Using organizational designs and practices that encourage autonomous action by employees, including work procedures, areas of responsibilities, and goals.
- *Team Accountability*: Ensuring that both decision-making authority and performance accountability reside in teams.

By sharing power with the employees, the idea is they can organize their work in a way which suits them to achieve the business objectives successfully because the information, communication and work streams, flow better and consequently are more efficient and effective. However, we have seen in Chapter 1 that the information and communication flows are full of flaws and that the work flows are not functioning seamlessly and fluidly, albeit the new methodology or best practice implemented. Empowering under such circumstances will be challenging to say the least. Of course, it is exactly the very reason to empower but the prerequisite for success is that information is shared by top management, as identified in the first bullet point, boundaries are clearly established and communicated and teams take and feel the collective responsibility. This is often not the case. Additionally, empowerment doesn't take the (end) responsibility away from top executives.

Going back to the previous quote from Kets de Vries: "Leaders under pressure also tend to delegate more work to subordinates and, if the pressure increases, may resort to bullying and threatening in order to meet the requirement for faster or better performance."

Since we live in an environment where speed to do business is always increasing, where, as a consequence, the pressure to perform increases constantly and where the work has to be done by fewer people the pitfall is very present that the benefits of empowerment go down the drain and that actually employees end up with more stress and frustration. Top executives will also end up frustrated and under even more pressure. Empowerment looks nice on paper and is a term readily uttered but it can be tricky business and will only work if top management actively enables it and if the organizational culture enhances it.

Obtaining and fostering a culture where creativeness and innovation are present means there is an environment where employees and employers feel safe and supported. This implies a setting where mistakes can be made, where people can talk about their doubts and misgivings and where they know they are appreciated and respected for their contributions.

Errors, failures, ineffective and inefficient workflows are easily identified and commented upon but how often do organizations celebrate their successes, milestones achieved, a job well done, a meeting well presided over, a presentation well-presented and a (major) effort successfully accomplished?

To continue with Kets de Vries, but now from his book *The Leader on the Couch*:

> Senior executives need to offer their subordinates not only praise when it's due, but also the perspective that making mistakes (though not repeating them) is part of any successful corporate culture. The philosophy of the wise organization shouldn't be to punish smart mistakes. To 'fail forward' needs to be part of an organization's implicit cultural values. As the saying goes, people who don't make any mistakes aren't doing anything! Mistakes can offer great opportunities for learning and personal growth, and leaders need to help ... understand that their fear of failure is part of the human condition.

Perhaps it is wisdom to consider applying the philosophy of a wise organization to not punishing the companies which provide services or sell products to them or not punishing a difficult customer. To not punishing the consumer who buys and uses your products.

Lean IT identifies five dimensions which must be addressed, similar to the balanced score card, to be able to manage the delivery and support of services and products adequately. One of the five dimensions is the Customer. For a service provider to provide services to the customer with the quality which adds value to customer, perceived as such by that customer, and achieve customer satisfaction the organization needs to know what the customer wants and needs. The customer requirements and wishes are known as the Voice of the Customer. This voice must be heard, acknowledged and understood by the service provider. The choice regarding the requirements and wishes are expressed in what is called Critical to Quality and enables the service provider to know what it should deliver and what the most important variables are they must address and control. To be able to deliver that desired and needed value to the customer Lean IT highlights the importance of being continuously in touch, with on-going dialogue, with the customer.

The same principle can be used within organizations, whether they are service providers, customers or suppliers: what is the Voice of the Employees, either on tactical or operational level, heard by the top executives on strategic level? What are the needs and the wishes (to be able to perform) expressed in Critical to Quality elements which are essential for the creation of value (to be successful)? Is there an on-going dialogue between strategic, tactical and operational level to make this happen? On-going dialogue means the internal information and communication streams need to flow, but in Chapter 1 we saw those are wanting. Internal stagnated flows will lead to external inconsistencies and flaws. If we want to improve customer satisfaction, we will have to start within the organization, including the practice of listening to the voice of the employee, because in the end, they make it happen. If we want to understand where the "resistance" for change comes from, listening to the voice of the employee on the various organizational levels will clarify and help a great deal. And if we want to be able to make the right decisions for the good of the company within the context of the overall common good, we might want to include the art of listening to the Voice of our Inner Self.

Staying with Lean, the core dimension is Behavior and Attitude. They define and maintain the organizational culture so the question is what kind of behaviors and attitudes an organization is rewarding and punishing. And if these are benefiting the organization in the long run or if they are creating an environment which will not enable healthy growth and in extension, a healthy corporate dynamic and (economic) system. With constructive and (morally) sound rewards, a clear message is being conveyed and a culture is being created. Are we constructing an organizational culture which is subsequently projected into the outside world and which therefore helps create the reality we want or are we constructing something else altogether, an organizational culture, a way of doing business which helps maintain or worse, deteriorates and poisons the economic and corporate reality? We should ask ourselves within which kind of environment we want professionals to create, and what influence the environmental condition has on what is being created. Is it possible to create a service, benefit from AI, introduce a new smart product for the common good if it has been created within an ill environment, for an ill system? What added value will best practices, methodologies or frameworks have if they operate within that unhealthy system, are introduced to maintain an unhealthy system?

We keep on introducing new frameworks and methodologies as a panacea we expect will prepare us for the new developments in the ICT world. From my management of change perspective and having seen and participated actively in organizational changes and transformations, the crux lies in how to initiate, manage and go about those changes (with a high degree of emphasis on people, human interaction and organizational culture), and not so much on the mere introduction of the new process, the new best practice, the new method. Looking as objectively and rationally as I can, my observation is that we are not doing the right thing, right, **right now**, so it just adds up; a broken and/or incomplete way of working, a non-constructive and fearful attitude and behavior are stacked on top of the new "super" development, structure or model. As long as we do not address the elephant in the room: psychological awareness, psychological growth, insight and related moral and ethical issues; as long as we don't address the premise of the business dynamic and system we have created and maintain, nothing will change for the better, even though the best practice or methodology per se are beneficial.

Top management has a big responsibility. They have a direct impact on the forming of organizational culture and on the way business is done. They are responsible and accountable. The more aware, the more conscious, the more psychological insight they have, the more consciously they can make decisions which are not triggered by unknown personal unfinished business or trauma and inner misbalance, the more balanced and informed decisions they can make. A balanced perspective of themselves can help them consciously decide how they wish to operate in the world. How do they wish to manage?

Have we *consciously* created a system and working dynamic—with long hours, few free days, constant pressure and deadlines—so we reach the end of the day exhausted and not wanting to think, but to just hang on the couch, consume TV and fast food and not think or reflect? Too (pre)occupied, too stressed out, too worried, too distracted to actually live in the moment and do our work and live our lives with awareness, with energy and with satisfaction? Are we living a conscious life or are we going through the motions of living and of working, pleasantly distracted from ourselves and the difficult ethical questions and moral dilemmas by constant back (and fore)ground auditory and visual noise provided by smart tech? Are we creative, energetic, happy and proud professionals or dazed and dulled corporate zombies?

We have maneuvered ourselves into an uncomfortable and painful chokehold of our own making: we have created an organizational and economic system where the highest value is making products which don't last, manipulating people into desiring new products in ever shorter replacement cycles; where the producers' demands and desires override the needs of consumers and where making money and spending has been made the reason for existing; where the norm has become you live to work and where morals and ethical business interactions are in a dire condition; where we have reached the point we cannot be proud of our (ICT) work and where there is a lot of stress. Why persist with this? This unhealthy system which has gone global with the "help" of technology, is not doing anyone any favors, quite the contrary. We have created this reality; let's create another one.

MORAL BURNOUT AND ETHICAL OBSOLESCENCE

The prevailing approach to organizational management, transformation and decision making is still based on the assumption and conviction that it is human rationality, the mechanistic linear thinking process which will lead to the solution and best choice after weighing, with deliberation, the pros and cons of a situation. The previous chapters have shown that is not the case and that non-rationality defines the behaviors and work patterns much more in organizations than we wish to admit. We have difficulty admitting it because it implies we are not as in control as we would like to be and not as all-knowing as we think we are or on the winner side of the list.

We are so afraid of non-rationality that we have categorized the non-rational state as inferior, unwanted and to be avoided at all costs. We have placed non-rationality on the other side of the list, the "wrong" side, the loser side. Therefore, the human (body) is a machine, the economy a wired system in which buttons can be pushed and consumers, apart from the service providers, make rational choices as well. In organizations, it is propagated executives make rational choices after careful and thoughtful deliberation.

Seeing the strong emotions displayed nowadays in everything we do, and instantly visible to all for consumption with the "help" of social media, the organizational and societal cultures are displaying a misbalanced environment: from seemingly rational we are on the other side of the spectrum: over the top emotions expressed as perceived offence, anger, frustration and sadness: emotions which have to be shared by the bigger the group, the better, to give those emotions outlet and the validity we need in our eyes.

Due to our efforts of trying to push away non acceptable emotions and thoughts to the depths of our psyche, they come out and express themselves with a vengeance, with extra vigor, with the help of social media. Out of control thoughts and out of control emotions because we are not conscious, balanced people in thought and emotion.

Because we have not addressed and given feelings, either pleasant or unpleasant, space for expression and acknowledgment we have disrespected and not given enough attention to an inherent aspect of our human beingness and of people in a greater context, in groups, organizations, societies and nations. Pleasant emotions are acceptable (up to a point) but unpleasant ones are deemed unwelcome and are put in the category of the loser side of our duality/polarity way of thinking.

In van Kets de Vries' *Coach and Couch*, in the section Going beyond Rationality: Decoding Deep Structure we read:

> Many leadership coaches, business practitioners, and scholars still subscribe to the myth that it is only what we see clearly (in other words, what is conscious) that matters. Assumptions made by economists about human rationality, and the models of learning and behavior modification developed by behavioral psychologists, have evolved into elegant, parsimonious, and measurable explanations for the way people act. For far too many people, the spirit of the economic machine seems to be chugging away in organizations—although the existing repertoire of 'rational' concepts has proven time and again to be insufficient to untangle really knotty individual and organizational dilemmas.

This ties into the mechanistic frameworks/best practices etc. and explains why transformations fail so often. Now there is a lot of talk about digital transformations and what CIOs must do. Are they prepared, equipped, psychologically speaking, for the challenge? Is top management capable of leading transformations and changes? To be fit to lead the transformation is not achieved by attending a lecture or doing a one-day course on change or transformation management. It implies taking the plunge into your own deep waters and shining the light on your own unconscious thought and feel processes. It is even suggested (CIO daily, 27/11/2018: What it takes to be a true CIO) CIOs could function as a type of coach to the other C-suite executives. Just because the transformation, or to use another word "mutation," is ICT induced, it doesn't mean the other C-suite executives mustn't be as prepared and skilled, be as conscious and as aware. Even more so, I would say, to be able to assess adequately if the mutation by technology is going in the desired direction.

As a cautionary observation and advice from an expert on organizational change, once again I would like to quote from van Kets de Vries' *Leaders on the Couch*:

> Because organizational neurosis is rooted in personal neurosis, organizational change is predicated on personal change. Thus leaders have to learn to challenge their habits and limitations, and act from real choice. Such a confrontation is the only way to not repeat the past. As has been said a number of times in this book, leaders who hope to change need to learn what drives their inner world; they need to recognize the salient themes in their inner theater. To change responses and behaviors in their external world, they need first to change what's happening in their internal world. When they see how hard it is to change themselves, they'll be more aware of the challenges that lie ahead in changing others. The good news is that, as leaders change, other will change as well. Mahatma Gandhi had some wise words on the topic of change: "We but mirror the world. All the tendencies present in the outer world are to be found in the world of our body. If we could change ourselves, the tendencies in the world would also change. As a man changes his own nature, so does the attitude of the world change towards him. This is the divine mystery supreme. A wonderful thing it is and the source of our happiness. We need not wait to see what others do.

As leaders change, they change the organizational dynamics, the interactions with their customers and suppliers and collectively they change the corporate dynamics and the economic system.

The quote indicates that leaders must learn to challenge their habits and limitations. People and organizations function because they have habits, or routines, which help them achieve their business objectives. Routines are structured into work flows, streamlined into processes, which when working well, help obtain the business outcomes. These established patterns clarify for all parties involved how to work and within which context. Therefore, if we wish to improve it makes a lot of sense to optimize and tweak those workflows. However, not all habits and routines are structured, or even identified as such. We are often not aware of them and hardly ever think of them consciously, to see if they are benefitting us and adding value to the customer, to the service provider, to the supplier. This is simply the way the work is done. The organizational habits and patterns however, especially when we are not aware of them, can make our organizational life and interactions more difficult and even sabotage a good working relationship or work flow. In summary, if we want to introduce a change to an organization or if a transformation is necessary a change in (thinking) habits and work patterns is called for.

In *An Evolutionary Theory of Economic Change* by Dr. Richard Nelson and Dr. Sidney Winter, published in 1982, the authors studied how organizations worked and concluded that: "Much of firm behavior," is to be "understood as a reflection of general habits and strategic orientations coming from firm's past," rather than "the result of a detailed survey of the remote twigs of the decision tree." Charles Duhigg cites these authors in his book *The Power of Habit* and continues with his clear exposition on how habits are formed, and how they can be changed. He clarifies: "… it may seem like most organizations make rational choices based on deliberate decision making but that's not really how companies work at all. Instead, firms are guided by long-held organizational habits, patterns that often emerge from thousands of employees' independent decisions. And these habits have more profound impacts than anyone previously understood."

If, as Nelson and Winter have noted, much of firm's behavior is a reflection of general habits and strategic orientations coming from the firm's past, an understanding of the organization's history, of its long-held habits and orientations are crucial if the organization wants to change or transform successfully. It would mean studying and understanding which habits and which behaviors were and are fostered, either with reward or punishment. Over time the rewarded (thinking) habit and consequently the punished (thinking) habits define the organizational culture.

In the previous chapter the high percentage (around 70%) of failed change trajectories in the ICT world was addressed. Although the percentage cannot be pinpointed on this number, and might be less (or more), organizational transformation failures are high and usually cost a lot of money, apart from the effort. These failures might have been reduced to a much lower percentage if the organizational past had been taken into account. From my own organizational change experience, the history of an organization is practically never considered, and only known to the people who have worked there for a long time and lived it personally. The past does have an impact and influences how business is conducted currently and in the future, and potentially negatively, if not understood.

If we look at the Bermuda Triangle situations as described in chapter one; the sluggish and flawed communication, information and work flows; if we look at the unhealthy economic system we have created and are operating in, I would say organizations, and consequently, professionals are suffering from accumulated organizational trauma.

Organizations are in a perpetual change mode and want to change with such speed they expect their employees to just get on with it and adjust, transform and be productive. The speed has become unnatural in the sense it doesn't permit the individuals of a company, a group or team, a department and in the widest scope, the whole organization, to cope with the changes. This leads to crisis and anguish.

An example is when colleagues who are fired due to economic circumstances or circumstances perceived as unjust. Additionally it is very important how the person is laid off, if it was done with respect. And what about a takeover? This can lead to stress with the professionals of the company taken over, and how the relationship plays out and is handled by the one taking over. A completely different way of working, overhaul of work routines meaning major adjustments, also in relation to locations, such as having to move to a different city or office. If these issues which can be perceived as unsettling and threatening are not addressed with care it can lead to considerable strain: constant changes, never giving professionals the time to settle a bit or to get used to a new way of working. Uncertainty about the next step, the next development, about your future, what is expected … if this is a constant it can lead to cumulative trauma.

The obvious trauma inducing elements are there as well: a bullying boss, undermining colleagues, a constant bombardment of negative comments, only negative feedback and hardly ever constructive recognition and constant pressure which can enhance fear of failure and unworthiness.

And last but not least, the agony due to questionable or unethical business interactions. If professionals are induced to design, develop, build, test and implement products or services which they know are flawed, not what the customer asked for, or programmed to fail at a predefined moment; if they have to work in an environment, a system where delivering value to the customer and the customer being satisfied is not very high on the priority list, a professional can wonder what the point is of his studies, his efforts and his sacrifices. This can cause stress and even trauma; a sort of (professional) existential crisis because the question is: what is the point? What am I doing? What kind of person/professional am I?

We already saw the neurosis present in organizations. Working in a neurotic organization long enough can eventually cause trauma with particular people or groups or create stress on an organizational scale.

The corporate neurosis and strain is reflected in how capitalism as we know it today has "evolved" into the duality based planned obsolescence reality we now live in. We are living our neurotic and traumatic "dream," or more accurately stated, nightmare.

There are few books on organizational trauma and even fewer which provide hands-on advice and tools to tackle it. An illuminating book on the topic, however, is written by Pat Vivian and Dr. Shanna Hormann, both with extensive experience dealing with trauma in non-profit and profit organizations. Their book *Organizational Trauma and Healing*, published in 2013, is focused on the trauma within non-profit organizations but this can be equally applied to profit organizations, as we shall see. In the introduction they write:

> The relationships that develop among the main aspects of organizational life—individual, work, and culture—are mutually reinforcing. That mutual reinforcement, together with the nature of highly mission-driven entities, generates and maintains an intense intellectual and emotional atmosphere. In a positive way this reinforcing triangle helps the organization stay true to its mission and solidify the rapport and bonds of its members. In a less productive way this intensity and mutual reinforcement are vehicles for transmission of trauma into the organization and among its members.

They address the three aspects of the triangle in more detail and in Chapter 8: Paying Attention to Organizational Patterns, they zoom in on patterns that can create trauma:

> Though many highly mission-driven organizations do not suffer from current or unhealed traumas, their cultures are still influenced by the nature of their work. Many have enduring cultural effects related to the organization's creation or may be at risk for cumulative trauma. Even in the most positive situations, where there is no evidence of trauma, it is important for organizations to pay attention to their internal workings. For an organization's health and sustainability, its members have to be able to see the organization clearly, to pay attention to enduring patterns and emerging dynamics, and name systemic facets that need to be addressed.

In profit organizations, the nature of the work is generally oriented at profit. The patterns and dynamics are structured in such a way, efficiently and effectively, they enable the realization of that ultimate goal: the sale of their product or service. The culture is influenced, as we read in the citation, by the nature of their work, by the patterns which originated in the past and endure. Are the patterns constructive and positive or have they created and are they still creating (consciously or unconsciously) trauma and are we projecting (consciously and/or unconsciously) that trauma into the world?

Do ICT organizations have patterns which have led and still lead to traumatization? Do those three main aspects of organizational life—individual, work and culture—get the attention they need in this fast-paced environment and are they in balance? Is the environment within ICT companies safe and open enough to have an honest and profound look at historical and current patterns and if they are adding value, if they are healthy? We don't question the business patterns enough, because we don't reflect (enough) and because we are transfixed, frozen to the spot as rabbits staring into the ICT lights and sounds. We take it as it is. We have been taught these patterns of thinking and approaching life as a de facto (double entry) reality.

Unhealthy patterns are unlikely to bring forth healthy products or services, an unhealthy business environment is unlikely to encourage healthy (inter)actions. Nearly every day we can read about unethical business practices regarding customers' data and information which the (tech) companies should be handling with utmost discretion instead of abusing the very trust put in them.

Is it ethical when "top" executives who were responsible for debacles within their company and who have caused misery for many, many people-think of the financial crisis of 2008 and the current shady practices of big tech companies—are still paid huge bonuses? What message is being conveyed? F**k it up, no problem, you will be handsomely awarded for it. Whereupon these people enter the circuit of non-executive managers or "advisors" for other companies. What is that about?

Saying you didn't know and are sorry when your "customers" data has been abused and not protected adequately and handled ethically doesn't cut it. As a CEO, founder or other C-suite level individual you are ultimately accountable and responsible for the way your company does business. Saying sorry publicly because there is an audience, but persevering in the same unethical practices is an attempt to wash your hands in innocence. You don't want to know, but you do, so you will be held to account. The fact is, if it hadn't become known, you would have happily persevered without skipping a heartbeat.

The tech companies say a lot of sorry nowadays and promise improvements. At the same time the new mantra is digital transformation, disruption, AI and virtual reality. They have opened Pandora's box, stand on the side with their hand on the upright lid and peer into the box with fascination to see what else comes crawling or flying out. Their myth-maniacal ideas about their role in our world is as astonishing as it is dangerous and nefarious.

In Chapter 9: Leading in Times of Organizational Trauma of Vivian's and Hormann's *Organizational Trauma and Healing* they are clear about the role, influence and therefore responsibility, of leaders:

> Leaders are critical in helping to heal traumatized organizations. While they cannot always protect an organization from trauma, leaders can help protect the organizational culture from traumatization. Their interpretation of events as well as their approach and actions strongly influence the dynamics within their organizational cultures. A leader's approach may be a mitigating factor, promoting healing within the organizational culture, or it may exacerbate the negative impacts of the situation and potentially threaten the future of the system.

Leaders will have to choose if they want to mitigate or exacerbate, but that does require understanding of their organization's past, the active patterns and habits, the factors influencing the culture and their own role in the system.

Leaders will have to tap into different, hidden and (mostly) neglected, aspects of themselves to lead in current and future times. (ICT) companies cannot place themselves outside the greater context of the societies and environments they function in and ignore and not want to know the impact they have on those societies. If companies are happy to take consumers' money, what do they give back?

In which direction do leaders of (ICT) organizations wish to take their companies and which values do they consider important? The choice will define what we keep sowing and reaping and if in the end it will benefit the common good or not. Will leaders step up to the challenge?

Bernard Burnes in Chapter 16 about management roles and responsibilities in *Managing Change* phrases it well:

> As the discussion of sustainability, diversity and ethics shows, however, globalization also raises crucial questions about the role and impact of organizations on and in a global society. These questions go beyond the traditional business concerns such as profit and loss, value for money or market share; they are concerned with fundamental issues of the role of organizations in sustaining life on Earth, respect for human diversity and dignity, and the ethical rules by which we live … All big organizations and many small ones now have policies on minimizing their environmental impact, promoting and managing diversity, and

behaving in an ethical fashion. Nevertheless, the gap between ethical rhetoric and the reality of unethical behavior seems to be getting wider rather than narrower. The real challenge for organizations is to change managerial behavior so that business ethics become business practices. Policies, skills and good intentions are clearly not enough. The fundamental point is managers need to behave differently. They need to put the policies and skills into practice.

Can we conclude that the widening gap between ethical rhetoric and ethical behavior is alarming? That we live in a world of business practices where the policies, skills and the patterns initiated in the past have grown into present day practices which have systematically phased out moral deliberations and principles, ethical practices and behavior in the name of profit and loss, value for money or market share?

We have fed, fostered and rewarded unethical habits and practices which have led to unethical practices in corporations on a global scale. We create neurotic organizations where sound morals are not rewarded but where unethical practices are condoned because the reward is money and power. This way of being and doing has led to a total ethical bankruptcy. The capitalism as we enact it today is based on a cynical planned obsolescence strategy and on the adoration of the making and spending of money. We do this under the guise of some higher value we are pursuing but in reality it has gone and continues going hand in hand with a planned obsolescence of ethics.

This moral opting out has led to destructive ego-driven attitudes and behaviors that flourish and take over our way of doing business and which have not only created a lot of waste in terms of tangible trash being dumped far from the shores where first the benefits were enjoyed but also other kinds of waste. Lean identifies eight types of waste, Muda, which can cause inefficient and ineffective operations: Transportation, Inventory, Motion, Waiting time, Overburden, Over processing, Defects and Rework. These are all wastes which, from the customer's perspective, do not add value. They are, in Lean terms, non-value-add activities or practices. I will go into more detail on these wastes in the next chapter but here, considering the moral and ethical discourse, I would like to introduce the dimension of psychological waste.

Just as the prior eight wastes mentioned which need to be eliminated so that the value streams within organizations can flow and create value-add, psychological waste, another non-value-add element, should be eliminated to enable healthy and ethical thinking and acting to take place. Psychological waste in this context refers to the unconstructive, ego-driven attitudes and behaviors which have fueled the patterns and practices of planned obsolescence and the duality approach expressing itself in an us versus them mentality and business dynamic. If we know what our own psychological waste is, obtained by shining our light on our inner world, we will be capable of getting rid of those elements which poison our own minds and actions. Becoming aware of the thoughts, feelings and unknown neurosis and/or trauma which lie beneath the surface and eliminating those unhealthy aspects of ourselves means we will be enacting/crystallizing something altogether different into perceivable reality. How dedicated are we to our own inner cleaning and weeding?

I will quote from Kets de Vries' *The Leader on the Couch*, adding between brackets and in cursive my own comments. "All of us need to realize that we take two journeys, one external and one internal. The way we experience the internal journey determines how we conduct and perceive the external journey. No matter how hard we work for success, if our thoughts are saturated with fear of failure (and of success) (*and any other kind of fear such as failure of being liked, followed or admired*) that negative thinking will kill whatever we attempt, making success impossible. When we know how to read and understand what happens inside us, when we recognize what we stand for, we don't have to depend so heavily on the reactions of others. If constructive thoughts are planted and cultivated in our inner theaters, positive outcomes will result."

We could state that where there is a will, there is a way. If we desire to change, if we need to transform organizations and be prepared for future challenges we will have to know ourselves. Kets de Vries continues with: "To acquire inner peace, to become more in touch with ourselves and oust our imposturous selves (*our ego*), we need to take a journey into ourselves. We need to learn to feel good in our skin, not assume the skin of others. Only by doing so are we able to live a life in our own way rather than the way we think others want us to. To come full cycle: if we hope to manage and overcome the impostor syndrome, we need to realize that success and achievement imply liking ourselves, liking what we do and liking how we do it (*and liking the desired end result*). We also need to learn that success isn't the key to happiness. On the contrary, happiness is the key to success!"

Know thyself and like what you see. Cho's words come to mind again: Go see, Ask Why and Show Respect. Go See your inner world and how it translates into the outside world and ask yourself if you like the translation; Ask Why you are doing the things the way you do and what you could and should change; Show Respect and listen to your inner voice, your employees' voice and the voice of your customer.

We can enforce and introduce auditing, oversight, more control etc. but that is only a check on behavior and habits. Nothing will change if *people*, internally, don't change. If we look at all the scandals, the fraud, the stealing of information, the selling of it, the manipulation and influencing for pure greed and power, no degree of oversight and committees are going to halt those practices. The economic and corporate way of doing business are indicators of our development as human beings: this is our creation. What have we created and what do we continue feeding?

We need to address our attitudes, our principles, our values. If a company has done this and expresses these in a positive, constructive and healthy manner, extensive oversight would not be necessary to the degree we are seeking now. And the fact is we cannot check and control everything; trust that business is done in a decent way must exist if healthy interactions are what we want. We have reached the point of no trust, where we must always be suspicious, expect the worst and cover not only our backs but our front and sides as well. Who wouldn't become paranoid like that? Are we becoming or are we already a paranoid society?

We have reached the state where profound hypocrisy reigns and taking the mickey out of customers, service providers, suppliers and trusting people has become the norm. What does that say about the values we uphold and our (inner) development and growth? It is time we all take responsibility for what we do out there, what we do in here. What we do to others. It is time to hold ourselves to account and to hold institutions, companies and governments to account. The sorry state of affairs doesn't just apply to the ICT world.

The lack of doing the inner work, of self-knowledge and self-correction has led to moral bankruptcy. The unease this causes within us: the disappointment with ourselves and with others, the anger (with ourselves and others), the frustration with ourselves and with others, are projected into the outside world as we have learned to interpret it: it is the fault of the other, the danger is the other, the other is the cause of all our woes. We feel unease, anger and frustration with a system we have collectively created which sees and treats people as collateral damage: a sign of a neurotic, deeply traumatized society.

We see a society with expressions of collective trauma due to an economic and corporate system which instead of fostering well-being is utilized against us. We are collectively traumatized by the (rapid) aggressive attacks on our livelihood, wellbeing and happiness. We are undermining and sabotaging our own sustainability and happiness.

Only collective moral force can unite the world

I Ching Hexagram 45—Ts'ui/Gathering Together

May the Force be with you

Star Wars

4

The Way Forward

Imagine, a value-based economic business model
Psychological waste
What to do with all these frameworks and models
Responsibility and Accountability ... oh dear

IMAGINE, A VALUE-BASED ECONOMIC
BUSINESS MODEL

It would be nice to take a magic wand in our hands, wave it with best intentions and cast a wondrous spell to solve all our problems with one sweep. Alas, reality is not like that. We will have to make more of an effort if we want to change the way we are doing things. And we must change, because we are on an unhealthy path, mentally, emotionally and physically, on a personal, corporate, national and planetary scale, we hard-headedly persist on going about our (business) lives the way we are doing now, asking for increasingly more trouble.

This chapter gives a few suggestions of what we could do. In which direction, according to me, we could tackle the issues discussed in the previous chapters. Ideas and options are launched for your reflection and contemplation.

Where to start? We saw that the Anglo Saxon capitalist system as we know it today, where planned obsolescence of quality and desirability are leading, where producers are to be catered to by willing and spending consumers, where the shortening of the replacement cycle is accelerated with increasing speed, where money has become our highest value and ethics have become the exception and finally, where human beings are considered and treated as collateral damage. We have seen how this type of system has negatively influenced internal organizational dynamics as well as the interactions between service providers, customers and suppliers. This system is in need of an overhaul and a reinvention. The disruptive transformations we like to talk about so much are needed for this bankrupt system as a whole.

We saw how double entry registration of finances, the quantification of practically everything we do and the duality perspective on (business) life has led to a myopic view of life based on the value money, and has distanced us from (even) seeing the other values which are crucial for healthy (business) interactions: honesty, integrity, probity, authenticity, humility, dignity, justice, etc.

We will have to go back to basics: what are our values? What do we consider important? What kind of (business) life do we want to create together, how do we want to interact, act, think, feel and be in such a way that the common good is considered, not only our own? Is the saying not: treat others the way you want to be treated? Together with *knowing and recognizing* the values we hold dear, going beyond an us and them and winner and loser duality look on life, it is the *acting on* those values which implies constant moral and ethical decisions and being true to them. If we want healthier and more respectful and constructive business interactions and dealings, a new committee for oversight, ethical codes, the new framework, next version of the best practice and the new awesome ICT developments are not going to bring these. They will be band aids, temporary fixes and even distractions on the surface as long as the deeper, core issues are not tackled; those are: our values, the (business) system and reality we have created and *our* role in that creation. If we want to change or improve anything, we will have to go from the inside out and tackle the most difficult task of all: ourselves.

Since our outside world is a reflection of our inner state of affairs, and the solution or improvements, if you prefer the term, is from the inside out, this chapter will also go from the inside out. The way forward begins with the way inward; we will have a look at what we can do to address our inner landscape and what we can do to understand ourselves better, why we are as we are and what we project onto the outside world. If we like what we see and if we don't, what we can do to change. Everything is possible: where there is a will, there is a way.

To understand what drives us, the fear, it is important to understand within yourself where that fear comes from, what shaped you early on, what you have been taught, what you have learned and what drives your thinking, feeling and actions. Because this has led to the (unperceived) personal traumas and organizational ones, to personal and corporate neurosis, to the sick economic system we have created as a result. Because the collective personal story is acted out in the world and shapes it. The system needs a detox.

So what can help us to understand? Do we all need to lie down on the couch and be analyzed by a Dr. Freud? No, we can do it ourselves, standing in the street, sitting at our desk or lying in a bubble bath. Awareness of yourself, creating consciousness and knowing yourself (better) can be done everywhere, anytime and defines our actions out there. A psychological detox is needed, from the inside out. A personal detox, a team detox, an organizational/corporate detox, an economic system detox. Not a technical transformation but a psychological and ethical one.

If we want to change we will have to tackle the unhealthy dynamic of the Planned Obsolescence capitalist system we have created. In this system there are the producers and the consumers. Both contribute to creating and maintaining this system so both groups need to change. To understand how they could change we will zoom in on their respective roles within the Planned Obsolescence theater.

In the case of planned obsolescence of quality and looking at the producers' role we can be very frank: It is unethical and even illegal what they are doing. This practice should be abolished. It forces people to buy new products at an ever increasing rate (and price). It forces people into (the mindset of) having to make more money (at what/any cost?), because they have to buy a new product, because the one they had stopped functioning (at a fixed time). This producers' practice is making life difficult for a lot of people and even impossible. People have a basic human right to be able to purchase trustworthy products, which have not been designed to fail on purpose and whose quality is a joke (but their prices aren't). The big tech companies—and other types of manufacturers—cannot rely on their good reputation anymore; that reputation they built once upon a time due to the well designed, sturdy, made to last products.

The producers should also be held accountable for the waste they create. The waste that is dumped for their new product in countries who don't have the luxury position to choose to refuse it. The creation of waste and how we deal with it is unethical. The impact our waste—our laptops, tablets, PCs, phones, refrigerators, cars, etc.—has on the communities is something producers should be held accountable for as well. We talk endlessly about corporate social responsibility: if producers create products which endure there will be less waste.

Once again, it is a basic human right not to be fooled and taken advantage of in this planned way. And so we come to the consumers' role in the planned obsolescence of quality theater act. What can they do? How can they protect themselves from these shady practices? Who looks after their interests? They can wait for someone or some entity to do something or they can act themselves; this implies an entity or organism which represents them and which can halt the producers aggressive push and coercion tactics. An institution which protects the rights of citizens is the *ombudsman.*

The ombudsman goes back to the Swedish ombudsman of 1809 and has evolved as an institution to various types of ombudsman as we know it today. Professor of International Trade Law at the University of Alberta Dr. Linda C. Reif gives an explanation of the institution in her book The Ombudsman, Good Governance and the International Human Rights System: "The ombudsman is a public sector institution, preferably established by the legislative branch of governance, to supervise the administrative activities of the executive branch. The ombudsman receives and investigates impartially complaints from the public concerning the conduct of government administration."

Currently, the ombudsman is also present in private organizations albeit not in many. The intention, however, is the same as the role of the institution in the public space. Dr. Reif further states: "The ombudsman is a mechanism which enhances transparency in government and democratic accountability, with the result that it assists in building good governance in a state. Also, some ombudsman institutions are hybrids. One variation is the human rights ombudsman which has both administrative oversight and human rights protection functions. With other variations, ombudsmen may be given mandates including anti-corruption, leadership code enforcement and/or environmental protection functions. Further, even the classical ombudsman can and does resolve some complaints with human rights aspects. Thus, both classical and human rights ombudsman institutions play roles in domestic human rights protection and promotion. The human rights norms involved may be derived from the international human rights obligations of the state concerned, with the result that the ombudsman acts as a domestic non-judicial institution for the implementation of international human rights law."

ICT companies operate on a global level and have a global impact. They are increasingly defining our way of working and living and becoming omnipresent in our private sphere. The rights of people, either in an organization or at home, need to be protected and transparency of ICT companies' business operations must be demanded and enforced. Furthermore, complaints by people need to be heard, addressed and acted upon, on a global level. Taking into account the flagrant abuse of big techs' position and the disdain for the privacy, protection and data of their "customers" worldwide, an institution such as the (human rights) ombudsman is a necessity. Perhaps (we have reached the point) the International Court of Justice is the safe and independent place under whose wing it could operate successfully and with enough clout.

Consumers can also protect themselves via consumer associations. Apart from advice, legal help and testing products these associations offer their members the opportunity to unite and have a stronger voice and position when dealing with producers. Perhaps an independent ICT Consumer Association is called for, not only to respond when the product has already been launched but to pro-actively have a say to avoid their interests being negatively impacted from the outset.

ISO norms can be used to safeguard a standard way of working which ensures making products and delivering services according to specifications to secure quality, safety and efficiency. ISO standards can be instrumental in facilitating International trade, as the ISO organization itself states on its website. It is an independent, non-governmental international organization with a membership of 162 national standards bodies.

There are numerous ISO norms for technology, ranging from compliance ISO 19600, Information Security ISO 27000 to norms for service delivery and support ISO20000. There is also an ISO for social responsibility ISO26000:2010. Unlike many other ISO standards, this last standard on social responsibility provides guidance rather than requirements and organizations therefore cannot be audited and certified. Which is a shame, because this is what we need nowadays. Although there will be companies who take the guidance to heart and act with a conscience, there are unfortunately too many examples—just open the newspaper—of organizations who do not take the guidance too seriously. Accountability, transparency, respect for stakeholder interests, the rule of law, international norms of behavior and respect for human rights all feature as the basic principles.

Customer organizations use the existence of ISO standards as a requirement for filtering the service providers they want to do business with. If a service provider doesn't have a specific ISO standard, it will not be considered for business. Maybe customer organizations should lay the bar higher regarding the requirements service providers and suppliers should comply with. Why not demand an ISO 26000 before even considering talking business? This would change the status of the standard to a norm that can be audited, not just a guidance which can be ignored. And the end users of the customer organization? If they are represented by an entity, they could demand the same compliance. Because the moment consumers refuse to consume, and specifically not consume their product, it is over and out for producers. Customers, and consumers, have much more power than they think.

And what if we had an ISO standard specifically for ethics? Why not audit an organization on their ethical practices and certify them, or not? Naturally, for it to be effective, we would need to audit more than just asserting the presence of an ethical code. Being ethical involves more than being in the possession of documents stating you are. Since ethics in the corporate environment and ICT are so wanting the time has come to draw the line on malpractices. And let's not convert the audit and obtainment of the certification into springing into action a month before the audit and producing the paperwork, but not acting upon the written word.

Considering the big tech companies sell you—your personal data— invade your privacy by tracking, linking information and wanting to know everything about you for the purpose of making money, and for power, power over you, citizens should push back on these practices. They, the companies, are violating our basic human rights.

What about the producers' and consumers' roles within the planned obsolescence of desirability context? We'll start with the consumers. The consumers must take a very, very hard look at themselves. What are the values you hold high? The newest watch—the bigger, the better—, the newest tablet, phone, laptop, headphones, etc … for what? To look cool, to be "in," a winner, to belong to the tribe? You do realize that you have been played by the producers? And if you don't buy, what will happen? What does it say about yourself if you need the newest of everything, immediately, and of course publish it on social media. What space does it fill?

What restlessness does it pacify? What fear does it divert? What are your values? Is this what life is about? Is it cool to be manipulated like a puppet on a string?

In the previous chapters the topic was discussed extensively and what it comes down to is to be aware of what drives you, what triggers you to buy, again and again. Shopping has become a pastime, an entertainment instead of an enterprise of acquisition because you need something. It is another form of distraction from yourself, from the scary inner universe of your thoughts and feelings and from asking yourself what your true values are and what makes you tick.

So how do we go about understanding our inner world and knowing ourselves, our values and being able to make independent, conscious decisions, on a personal level and in an organizational setting? There are many books on psychology which can help us understand ourselves better and according to our preference we can choose an approach we feel comfortable with. We saw in Manfred Kets de Vries' book *The Leader on the Couch* and *Coach and Couch* how closely the personal inner state and the one expressed in an organizational environment are related. A very pragmatic, recognizable and workable approach, on a personal as well as on an organizational level, is Transactional Analysis.

Transactional Analysis was founded by Eric Berne, M.D. (1910–1970). He wrote multiple books and the titles *Games People Play* (1964), *What do You Say after You Say Hello* (1971) and *Beyond Games and Scripts* (an anthology of his work, 1976) will perhaps ring a bell, since the first book was a bestseller for two years. Transactional Analysis really came into the spotlight when Thomas A. Harris, M.D. (and his wife Amy) wrote the book *I'm OK—You're OK* in 1967. In the words of the International Transactional Analysis Association:

> Transactional analysis is a social psychology developed by Eric Berne, MD (d.1970). Berne's theory consists of certain key concepts that practitioners use to help clients, students, and systems analyze and change patterns of interaction that interfere with achieving life aspirations. Over the past 40 years, Berne's theory has evolved to include applications in counseling, education, organizational development, and psychotherapy. Research studies have evaluated the effectiveness of transactional analysis in a wide variety of contexts … Organizational transactional analysts work in, or for, organizations using transactional analysis concepts and techniques to evaluate an organization's developmental processes and challenges as well as its dysfunctional behaviors.

Transactions are verbal as well as non-verbal interchanges between people and are therefore about communication. Organizational Transactional Analysis could help considerably with the issues described in chapter one regarding the difficult and/or stagnant communication flows top-down, bottom-up and transversal within the same organization as well as help with the communication (transactions) between service providers, customers and suppliers. The ICT environment doesn't exactly excel in constructive communications and awareness of the mechanisms present within themselves and with others, to put it mildly.

Transactional Analysis continues developing and is updated with new research and insight. The attraction and usefulness is the very pragmatic and recognizable ego-states and transactions described, analyzed and clarified which helps people on an individual level gain better understanding of themselves, but also helps groups and organizations gain knowledge on their group transactions, games played and scripts repeated, constructive as well as destructive ones. Berne specifically addresses group dynamics in e.g. his books *Structure and Dynamics of Organizations and Groups* (1963) and *Principles of Group Treatment* (1966).

This book is not the place to go deeper into the ins and outs of Transactional Analysis (TA), but for a basic understanding of the elements involved I will cite again from the International Transactional Analysis Association referring to the core concepts of TA.

Ego States

"Eric Berne made complex interpersonal transactions understandable when he recognized that the human personality is made up of three "ego states." Each ego state is an entire system of thoughts, feelings, and behaviors from which we interact with one another. The Parent, Adult and Child ego states and the interaction between them form the foundation of transactional analysis theory. These concepts have spread into many areas of therapy, education, and consulting as practiced today."

The three ego states are present within all of us and observable through behavior. Our inner Parent, Adult, or Child manifests itself and is e.g. noticeable by what is said and done. To give a brief explanation I refer to the descriptions provided on ericberne.com which include Berne's words as well:

"The **Parent** represents a massive collection of recordings in the brain of *external* events experienced or perceived in approximately the first five years of life. Since the majority of the external events experienced by a child are actions of the parent, the ego state was appropriately called Parent. Note that events perceived by the child from individuals that are NOT parents (but who are often in parent-like roles) are also recorded in the Parent. When Transactional Analysts refer to the Parent ego state (as opposed to a biological or stepparent), it is capitalized. The same goes for the other two states (Adult and Child). Examples of recordings in the Parent include:

"Never talk to strangers"
"Always chew with your mouth closed"
"Look both ways before you cross the street"

In contrast to the Parent, the **Child** represents the recordings in the brain of *internal* events associated with external events the child perceives. Stated another way, stored in the Child are the *emotions* or *feelings* which accompanied external events. Like the Parent, recordings in the Child occur from childbirth all the way up to the age of approximately five years old. Examples of recordings in the Child include:

- "When I saw the monster's face, I felt really scared"
- "The clown at the birthday party was really funny!"

The **Adult** is the last ego state. Close to one year of age, a child begins to exhibit gross motor activity. This is the beginning of the Adult in the small child. Adult data grows out of the child's ability to see what is different than what he or she observed (Parent) or felt (Child). In other words, the Adult allows the young person to evaluate and validate Child and Parental data. Berne describes the Adult as being "principally concerned with transforming stimuli into pieces of information, and processing and filing that information on the basis of previous experience." Stated another way, Harris describes the Adult as "a data-processing computer, which grinds out decisions after computing the information from three sources: the Parent, the Child, and the data which the adult has gathered and is gathering.""

Are we capable of perceiving which ego state is present when we interact with our colleagues, superiors, customers or partners and how that state is triggered and why?

Transactions

"Transactions refer to the communication exchanges between people. Transactional analysts are trained to recognize which ego states people are transacting from and to follow the transactional sequences so they can intervene and improve the quality and effectiveness of communication.

Strokes

Berne observed that people need strokes, the units of interpersonal recognition, to survive and thrive. Understanding how people give and receive positive and negative strokes and changing unhealthy patterns of stroking are powerful aspects of work in transactional analysis.

I'm OK—You're OK

"I'm OK—You're OK" is probably the best-known expression of the purpose of transactional analysis: to establish and reinforce the position that recognizes the value and worth of every person. Transactional analysts regard people as basically "OK" and thus capable of change, growth, and healthy interactions.

Games People Play

Berne defined certain socially dysfunctional behavioral patterns as "games." These repetitive, devious transactions are principally intended to obtain strokes but instead they reinforce negative feelings and self-concepts, and mask the direct expression of thoughts and emotions. Berne tagged these games with such instantly recognizable names as "Why Don't You, Yes But," "Now I've Got You, You SOB," and "I'm Only Trying to Help You."

Life Script

Eric Berne proposed that dysfunctional behavior is the result of self-limiting decisions made in childhood in the interest of survival. Such decisions culminate in what Berne called the "life script," the pre-conscious life plan that governs the way life is lived out. Changing the life script is the aim of transactional analysis psychotherapy. Replacing violent organizational or societal scripting with cooperative non-violent behavior is the aim of other applications of transactional analysis.

Contracts

Transactional analysis practice is based upon mutual contracting for change. Transactional analysts view people as capable of deciding what they want for their lives. Accordingly transactional analysis does its work on a contractual basis between the client and the therapist, educator, or consultant."

To a certain degree we can all recognize games we play with colleagues, our bosses, customers or suppliers. Do we play the same games all the time and are we aware of the script we play out over and over again? Which ego state is active when there is a transaction with a "difficult" customer: Parent, Adult or Child? Do we need constant recognition to feel worthy (strokes) and what is our basic stance in life, as presented in Harris' book:

1. I'm not OK—You're OK
2. I'm not OK—You're not OK
3. I'm Ok—You're not OK
4. I'm Ok—You're OK

Do we dare be honest and delve into our inner world and see which of the four life positions we hold? And how this position influences the relations we have with others? Harris' book and subsequent publications on the topic, also specifically related to transactions in an organizational context, are generally speaking eye-openers for those involved and help create awareness plus provide tools to come into the I'm OK—You're OK position. For we all tend to be in one of the first three, uh-oh!

Consumers, consumed by the desire to buy (I'm not OK—You're not OK or I'm not OK—You're OK or...?) and whose buttons are pushed by producers with the planned obsolescence of desirability tactics (I'm not OK—You're not OK or I'm OK—You're not OK..or?), could benefit from understanding what drives them to seek satisfaction in continuous acquisition and materialism and the need/urge to feel being part of a particular tribe.

Producers, consumed by the desire to sell (I'm OK, You're not OK or I'm not OK—You're OK, or..?), and whose sole stimulus is the quantified value of money depicted in profit, stakeholder value and growth with the use of planned obsolescence of desirability and quality (I'm OK—You're not OK, I'm not OK—You're not OK, or..?), could benefit from understanding what drives them to seek satisfaction in continuous selling and waste production, in a continuous accelerated pace and the need/urge to feel part of that particular tribe.

We can state that the misbalanced capitalist system we have created contains plenty of not OK positions. It's time to make a real effort to reach a healthy I'm OK—You're OK position and a balanced system.

Since change is achieved from the inside out and ICT organizations are in constant flux and in need of transforming, why not add courses in basic psychology, e.g. TA, to help the transformation and make it lasting and successful? It helps to improve relations, interactions, the transactions, and therefore the business performance. Why not offer trainings where a certification is not the primary goal, but understanding and in depth discussions are the focus? Where reflection is possible and where there is space for ah-hah moments.

Since we are on the subject, maybe a training on ethics wouldn't be a bad idea either. Let's talk openly about values and what the organization we work for stands for. For ICT companies discussions on the impact on society would not just be a good idea but should even be part of the curriculum. Washing our hands in feigned innocence of the global impact is not acceptable anymore.

If we want to understand more about what we put out there in the world, what we crystallize into being from the inside out, the Swiss psychologist and psychiatrist Carl Gustav Jung (1875–1916) can help us understand our projections. Jung uses analytic psychology and introduces concepts such as archetypes, the collective unconscious and extraverted and introverted personalities. Jung recognizes that unconscious processes have a significant effect on our behavior and identifies different reaction styles, such as introvert and extrovert. Introvert relates to a focus on our inner world, at expense of the outer environment with its social interactions and extrovert is more focused on living out inner dynamics through social interactions in the outer world.

Jung addresses the unconscious which, when not getting the right attention and outlet, can manifest itself in an unhealthy way, having been suppressed for too long. In Dr. Ira Progroff's book: *Jung's Psychology and its social meaning* (1973) we read:

> … under the press of modern social competition, the individual must make
> a particular effort to suppress his weaker functions. He deliberately cuts

them out of consciousness so that he can concentrate on the strongest function, that is, the function on which he can "capitalize." In doing this, however, he creates a very dangerous situation within his psyche, a situation of
unbalance … The weakest and least adapted function are taken over by the
Shadow (the unknown dark side of the personality) complex and becomes
identified with the negative, unpleasant side of the personality. The opposite of the conscious attitude reaches the surface, breaking in on consciousness as an autonomous "partial system."

Jung indicates that the shadow tends to psychological projection, where
we see in others the unpleasant or inferior traits we do not dare see or simply do not see in ourselves. The fears we have are projected into the others:
Us and Them and Winners and Losers.

What do we, service providers, project onto the other, onto the customer, and vice versa? What have we collectively projected into and unto
the outside world to have arrived at the Planned Obsolescence capitalist
system which is damaging our collective selves on all levels? Has our collective Shadow been so reinforced it acts with increasing frenzy to satisfy
its desires? Are we creating all we fear as a self-fulfilling prophecy because
we are not conscious of our inner functions?

Jung himself says in *Psychology and Religion* (1969): "All gaps in our
actual knowledge are still filled out with projections. We are still so sure
we know what other people think or what their true character is. We are
convinced that certain people have all the bad qualities we do not know
in ourselves or that they practice all those vices which could, of course,
never be our own. If you imagine someone who is brave enough to with-
draw all these projections, then you get an individual who is conscious of
a pretty thick shadow. Such a man has saddled himself with new problems and conflicts. He has become a serious problem to himself, as he is
now unable to say that *they* must be fought against. He lives in the 'House
of the Gathering'. Such a man knows that whatever is wrong in the world
is in himself, and if he only learns to deal with his own shadow he has
done something real for the world. He has succeeded in shouldering at
least an infinitesimal part of the gigantic, unsolved social problems of our
day. These problems are mostly so difficult because they are poisoned by
mutual projections. How can he see straight when he does not see himself
and the darkness he unconsciously carries into all his dealings?"

Modern society and the dynamics of (ICT) business dealings could do
with a Jungian view on how they come about and what the driving forces
are. Perhaps the Jungian experts need to use their voice a bit more and

shine their light on the current sorry state of affairs for the benefit of the common good.

In summary, apart from the abolition of the Planned Obsolescence capitalist system we have created, by prohibiting these practices by law, private citizens and employees of companies need protection and representation, need to protect themselves, with the help of e.g. the ombudsman, ISO norms and real oversight.

Where are the governments in all this? They are the organism and entity who have come into being to ensure an orderly, respectful and just cohabitation, taking into consideration the common good of all its citizens. Are they protecting and addressing the common values, general interests and common good of all they represent? Or have they been infected by the duality bug, been taken over by the sole value—money—, have they bowed to the quantification of our values and have they mutated into the facilitators of corporations and forgotten their role as representatives of the people who voted for them?

Are states protecting their citizens when they adopt and implement the new products and "services" ICT companies come up with which make it possible to link data, track and monitor a citizens' every move? Where he took the bus, at what time, where he got off and back on? Where she parked, what kind of a car she has, how long she parked, when she left? Are citizens' basic human rights protected with cameras on every street corner—a shouting example of feeding off fear and pushed with the planned obsolescence of desirability tactic—so that even where you walk, stroll, with whom, which pub you go to etc. is filmed, monitored and stored? Can states be considered complicit with ICT companies? Are they failing their duties?

GDPR, however, mandatory since May 2018, is an excellent example where the rights of people *have* been considered and have been acted upon. And it shows what the bundling of forces and interests can accomplish if and when we set our minds to it.

If governments aren't doing what they have been given a mandate for and if they are not acting on behalf of the common good, perhaps the time has come to hold them to account as well. Impossible? Not quite. There is an unprecedented example from The Netherlands, where the Urgenda Foundation won the case against the Dutch government on June 24, 2015 forcing it to adopt more stringent climate policies. Citing from Urgenda's website (urgenda.nl): "Urgenda and 900 co-plaintiffs won the climate case against the government, which is now required to take more effective climate action to reduce the Netherlands' considerable share in global emissions. This is the first time a judge has legally required a State to take precautions against climate change." Marjan Minnesma, co-founder and director of Urgenda and who initiated the court case against the Dutch state with a team of lawyers and the 900 co-plaintiffs in 2013 says of the verdict:

> All the plaintiffs are overjoyed by the result. This makes it crystal clear that climate change is a huge problem that needs to be dealt with much more effectively, and that states can no longer afford inaction. States are meant to protect their citizens, and if politicians will not do this of their own accord, then the courts are there to help.

What about an "Urgenda" against states who do not protect citizens from the Planned Obsolescence tactics of organizations? And from the big tech companies dealing in our personal data? From not protecting us against tracking and monitoring our movements and lying? Do we need an "Urgenda" to take action against the states' dereliction of duties in regards to citizens' basic human right not to be filmed, monitored and tracked, the basic human right for privacy? If governments do not snap out of their inaction and protect citizens or worse, are complicit to these practices, citizens can use the courts to protect themselves and to protect everything democracy stand for.

A call to change the capitalist system we have known for so long and have accepted as the way it is may seem an idealistic and impossible dream. It isn't, because, as we have seen in the previous chapters, we are the creators of the system and therefore we can change our creation if we so desire. But what should we replace it with and where should we put our directed energy?

In chapter two I talked about doing the right thing, right, the first time as opposed to doing something, faster and faster and entering a continuous cycle of error correction once it is implemented or just throwing it away or phasing it out. I introduced Dr. Klamer and his book *Doing the right thing, a value-based economy* as an alternative to classical money driven economics, as a different way of looking at economics and the values we strive to uphold, for ourselves and for the common good.

Based on the ancient Roman and Greek philosophers, Christian theologians and on more recent philosophers such as Alasdair MacIntyre, Martha Nussbaum, Philippa Foot (1920–2010) and McClosky, Dr. Klamer names the four cardinal virtues (these are internalized behavioral values) as identified by Aristotle in his Nicomachean Ethics, which, if we choose to, define our actions:

- *Prudence*: acting thoughtfully, cautiously, with foresight and taking into account the relevant circumstances.
- *Temperance:* doing not too much and not too little, knowing the right middle ground between extremes.
- *Courage*: overcoming fear to do the right thing.
- *Justice:* doing so with regard to the feelings and interests of others.

Christian theologians like Thomas Aquinas added the three theological virtues:

- *Faith:* trusting yourself, your intuition, your background, your karma, the supernatural God.
- *Hope:* trusting that some good will come from your action.
- *Love:* feeling deeply connected with the other, others and accepting the other as he or she is.

These seven virtues are a simplification of all they encompass but are presented in this manner to get a better grasp for comprehension purposes. I refer to the bibliography for further in depth reading. These virtues are the values we attribute to actions. In a personal and/or organizational context the values which we uphold need to be clear and shared, especially in the organizational environment, because they will define how employer and employee act (virtuous or not) and they will define and shape the organizational culture. The values will define if it is an accepted practice to arrive late to work, or to address the customer in a certain way or to design or test with prudence, temperance, courage and justice, or not.

If we strive for shared values to be expressed in our actions, and we agree we want to do what is right, what is important for us and important for the common good, we need to know which values we consider important and apply them with all the knowledge (inner and outer) we have. This is what Aristotle called phronesis, practical wisdom. I will repeat a quote I used earlier from Dr. Klamer:

> He (Gonzalo Bustamante) explains that it calls for thoughtfulness, awareness of the goods to strive for and the relevant values, and a clear understanding on what people want and need, proven practices and strategies (Bustamante Kuschel, 2012).

In short, you can state that phronesis is the virtue of making values real. Making values real is about doing the right thing; it is about having the courage to act on the values we share and consider important. It is your conscience speaking and you listening and acting on it.

When a new ICT product or service is being planned, designed, manufactured or developed, e.g. AI or another IoT, are the relevant circumstances thought of and taken into account (Prudence), is the plan or design solid and in balance and do we not want and do too much (Temperance), do we want to do the right thing and not cut corners (Courage) and do we create a product or service with regard to the interests of others (Justice)? Do we trust our inner voice and listen to our intuition (Faith), do we act in a way we trust will do good (Hope) and do we feel connected to the people who will eventually use our product or service (Love) and as a result of all these values we will plan, design, manufacture or develop a product or service that adds value, not only in monetary terms?

Phronesis is when you act with conscience in your business dealings. When you listen to the nagging feeling your decision to outsource to a particular party maybe wasn't the best idea, although they were the cheapest, when you should have shared the complete story with your customer to enable her to make a better, well-informed decision; phronesis is when you practice what you preach, when you realize what influence you have on the organizational culture, when you say no to certain practices that go against your … conscience? When you know your actions would hurt others, damage them and damage the company you work for and as a result you make a different choice.

Phronesis is not new, but it is forgotten. It has been phased out of the planned obsolescence capitalist system we have now. The seven virtues described here were common knowledge up to the nineteenth century. They were even taught in school. In the twentieth century the decline started and now we can state that they have mostly been sidelined and are even considered "old-fashioned."

Dr. Klamer says on the topic: "The idea of phronesis is quite different from the idea of rational behavior or rational choice that you learn about in standard economics. The idea rationality presumes that we can *calculate* the best choice; it involves the idea we can derive the best choice by maximizing some objective function (utility, profit) under certain constraints (income, prices and the like). Economists embrace the idea because it enables the modeling of decision making in the form of mathematical equations. The modeling gives an idea the aura of "science." The idea of phronesis makes us realize that too much is involved in doing the right thing, that calculation is therefore nigh impossible, and modeling quite hopeless. The process phronesis is difficult to trace, and hard to catch in the form of rules and (predictable) patterns …"

By converting decision making, based on the mechanistic, linear dualist worldview, into an exercise of calculus we have created the situation where we can distance ourselves from the values which are also very important, crucial, for harmonious cohabitation. We have created a shield of rationality behind which we hide so that we don't have to confront the difficult— moral and ethical—aspects of (business) life. We lack courage (or to put it more harshly: we are cowards).

To continue with Dr. Klamer: "The idea of rationality makes perfect sense in an instrumentalist interpretation of science. When economists embraced the goal of policy relevance, as they did in the thirties of the twentieth century, it made sense to assume that consumers, workers and businesses were rational. That assumption facilitates modeling of economic processes and the models that produce the results that presumably enable policy makers to conduct rational policies. At least, this was how the idea of rationality was presumed to work."

The assumptions and presumptions have proved to be wrong, or at least, far too narrow and limited. The toxic capitalist economic system we have now is the result of our tunnel vision approach concerning producers and consumers. The mere categorization of people into producers and consumers facilitates the dual approach and directs the focus to quantification of the producers' products and the consumers' consumption, as if that is all an economic system is about. It is then not difficult, but a small step, to ignore and forget values and virtues, morality and ethics. Welcome to the twenty-first century: modern man's achievements and "progress."

Phronesis, practical wisdom, comes from the inside out. Integrity, honesty, authenticity, probity and other (moral) values must return to the forefront of our (business) lives. Real leadership is having the moral authority to lead. Real leaders have the courage to make practical, wise decisions. Real leaders embody the values and stand up for them.

Values externalized into business dealings, into the way we communicate, into the manner in which information and data are used, forms the organizational culture. Apart from the inner work we must do, we must also change the pattern, the habits we have created and feed and continue creating and feeding. Changing our interior world will change our habits and change the corporate culture and interactions (transactions) with our customers and suppliers.

As Kets de Vries wrote: "The real challenge for organizations is to change managerial behavior so that business ethics become business practices. Policies, skills and good intentions are clearly not enough. The fundamental point is managers need to behave differently. They need to put the policies and skills into practice." The new practices, patterns, behaviors and habits will create a new corporate culture, and consequently change the business climate of the morally bankrupt economic system we have now.

Working from the inside out and changing a corporate culture requires courage. A bad habit is difficult to change, especially when the habit has taken on the proportions of addiction. The producers have to change their habit of designing, manufacturing and developing products which will fail at a predestined time; they have to change their habit of encouraging the addiction with their customers; they have to change their habit of manipulation, lying and fraud. Customers need to change their habit of not being able to say no, to craving purchases to give them the new high; they have to change the habit of being a lemming and dancing to the tune of the Pied Piper.

We saw previously that the Planned Obsolescence economic system needs an overhaul and we saw what the producers, customers and state role is in this dynamic. If an organization desires to change and really make a difference, their habits and organizational patterns need to be taken by the horns. There are many studies and publications on habits and how to change them. I cited from Duhigg's book *The Power of Habit* in the previous chapter. Duhigg explains how our habits are formed, and how to change them. Once again, it implies an understanding of our inner world and the cues which trigger a routine to achieve a desired result (the reward). He states that if you want to change habits, you have to change the routine (the physical, mental and/or emotional behavior that follows the cue automatically) because the cues will always be there and are outside your control and you still desire the reward, e.g. the business deal you want to win. What it comes down to is you can change your routine, the patterns, the behavior to achieve the reward. Winning a business deal is what business is about, but *how* do you win it? How do you treat your employees to achieve it, or your customers and suppliers? Are you honest, authentic, sincere? Do you wish to achieve the end result at all costs, do you ignore or push aside the common good, the moral questions? Duhigg's book is very useful but I would add that we should not take the reward as a given but that we should question the very reward we pursue. The economic system we have created with our habits over the years has put the achievement of money, power and status as the ultimate reward to strive for. Because supposedly these rewards make us happy and supposedly those are the values life on this planet earth is all about.

Our problem now is what we wish to strive for. Because our striving has led to habits which are unhealthy for ourselves and for others. Do we ever ask ourselves what we are doing here on planet Earth? What (business) life is about during our existence on this globe? What our behavior is on this planet: that of a guest or that of the host? We are guests of this living organism, for we will die and she will live on, but we act as hosts, bad ones at that, where we have given ourselves the right to shamelessly take and (ab)use as we see fit. Do we ever think of that or do we live in complete denial? What do we fear?

Do you, as a manager, walk around and observe? Do you talk to the people on all levels of your organization? Do you listen to them? Do you ever have a coffee, or lunch with them in the canteen? Do you mingle or keep the same company as always? Do you actually know your company: its habits, its patterns, its communication and information workflows? Would you be able to describe the organizational culture and do you ever wonder what your contribution is to that culture? Or are you also in denial about those topics?

Planned obsolescence of quality and desirability are toxic habits to which producers as well as consumers are addicted. Governments are addicted as well; they have adopted the system as the de facto standard of life, and even facilitate and enable it, to the detriment of the citizens they should protect. This opting out of (moral) responsibility has become blatantly visible. It is no surprise people are fed up.

PSYCHOLOGICAL WASTE

To create awareness and live a more conscious life with phronesis we need to detox. We need to eliminate psychological toxins as well as toxins in habits, patterns and behavior which define our (corporate) culture.

Lean (IT) names seven types of waste (Muda) we should eliminate. The origin of Lean is within the car manufacturing industry (Toyota) so the wastes identified refer to those activities. Lean IT has applied the

IT dimension to the wastes. Variations and additions to the classic seven types of waste have been introduced to address specific IT facets in other organizations. The wastes, activities using resources which do not add any value for the customer, known with the acronym TIMWOOD, are:

1. *Transporting (Time)*: the actual transportation of goods and materials within your facility. It is the time used for the movement of equipment, parts and also people between processes which can be considerable and is a non-value add activity, especially when processes and process flows are not understood or followed.
2. *Inventory*: the stock sitting in the warehouse and costing you money. This can also refer to e.g. IT tools and processes which have been acquired or defined but are not being used.
3. *Motion*: as Transporting, refers to movement, and therefore time, but is focused on the movement within/during the process, so the process and/or information flow itself.
4. *Waiting*: refers literally to waiting for someone, for information, for inputs, a decision etc. before you can continue. Waiting for people who come late to meetings and waiting for rescheduling of meetings.
5. *Over-processing*: when you do more than is required to respond to the customer expectation or agreement. This is often due to poor or unclear communication.
6. *Over-production*: as the term indicates, when you produce more than is required meaning you have put energy and time into something which was not necessary. Just in Time production and delivery aims to avoid the creation of this type of waste.
7. *Defects and rework*: correcting errors, having to do rework and incident resolutions can be very expensive. Doing it right the first time, is what Lean IT propagates.

These are seven types of waste categorized on a high level and we can name endless examples of non-value-add activities within the ICT sector: ICT departments within the same company with their own way of working instead of following a standardized approach, unclear information and communication flows, circumvention of workflows, attention to incident management which temporarily resolves an issue instead of solving issues structurally with problem management, poor or no quality control, not understanding customer requirements, promising things to customers you cannot deliver, multiple tools with a lot of overlap, despite the tools still doing a lot manually and not knowing and not being able to indicate what the ICT costs are, etc. In summary, not being in control, not having a grip and creating and working in waste.

These seven wastes, Muda, when applied to ICT, focus on the non-value add(ing) steps within processes (the work, information and communication workflows) and between the various flows where they interface. However, Lean also identifies other kinds of waste, just as important but undervalued, e.g. Muri. Muri can be translated as overburden. When wanting to eliminate the Muda wastes, we have to be careful not to demand too much from our employees and put too much pressure on them. If we do that, we can actually *create* Muda, instead of eliminating them. Examples of Muri are ill defined processes, unclear or non-existing procedures and/or work instructions, unclear communication lines or even contradictory messages, demanding employees to work according to a process, methodology or with tools they have not been properly trained in and office organization and layout which does not foster, or worse, even undermines performance and productivity. An ill equipped service desk or a coffee machine which produces something resembling dishwater instead of the wonderful invigorating brew it is supposed to be, are also Muri!

There is a third kind of waste, Mura. Mura means unevenness and refers to, e.g. an uneven, inconsistent, customer demand. This can upset the pace in the workflow. Mura can also apply to the organization internally, when you have to produce an on the spur report to management … and then it isn't even read.

If you really want to improve the performance of an organization you will have to tackle these three types of waste, but it is not enough improvement if you limit the waste elimination to processes, to the workflows. Since real and staying transformations come from the inside out and as we have seen in previous chapters what the lack of psychological insight and inner work has manifested into the outside world, we should eliminate the psychological waste as well if we are serious about improving. We have to weed our inner garden and get rid of the kind of waste that sabotages ourselves and our efforts to be more effective and efficient and to achieve the end result we truly desire according to healthier and constructive values. We can use the Lean wastes for this and add the psychological dimension to them:

1. *Time (Transporting)*: I would like to highlight the T as Time. Time we waste with unawareness of ourselves and of the organizational culture and dynamics. Time wasted on running around like

headless chickens, time usurped by the inner monkey mind chattering away about the other, the loser, time gone down the drain with the continuous craving for buying, spending and selling to feel fulfilled. Precious time wasted on negative thoughts and feelings and on feeding unethical and morally questionable practices. All this wasted time could be used to ponder, to think, to reflect and mull things over before the frenzied activity of doing, which gives the false sense of progress. Time to get and be in touch with your inner self and to become aware of your thoughts and feelings and what cues trigger which routines. Time to think about the reward you are pursuing on an organizational and personal level and time for practical wisdom, phronesis. Time to make wise decisions for the common good.

2. *Inventory*: This refers to the stock sitting in the warehouse and costing you money. Psychological waste would be the strengths and weaknesses you have within you but which you do not use or address. Which you do not even know. Which could have an enormous added value for yourself as well as for the organization you work for. Everyone has more than one talent, more than one strength. We tend to label ourselves and others in a certain manner, e.g. the KPI expert, and that is it, you always end up doing something with KPIs and are given no or hardly any opportunities to do something else and to develop and put to good use your other strengths and talents. And do you recognize and acknowledge your weaknesses or brush them under the carpet? It is no shame to have weaknesses, but it is a shame, a pity, not to address them. They can give you valuable information about yourself and help you grow if you wish to do so.

3. *Motion*: Do you know your inner thinking and feeling flows? Can you capture the moment when dark or negative thoughts with associated feelings start to stir within you? Are you aware how they manifest in your transactions and interactions with colleagues, customers and suppliers? Are you aware of your body language, facial expression and gestures through which they manifest? Know that inner flow and let the ego-flow go. Learn to direct that energy to something with value-add for yourself, and in consequence for others.

4. *Waiting*: This is the waste of waiting for someone else to have the courage to speak up, to say no, to address the difficult topics. Waiting for something or someone out there to solve the issues in here. We tend to wait for others to take the initiative to face unpleasant

situations, even our own. This is the waiting for Santa Claus to come and solve all.

5. *Over-processing*: This is the waste created by over-processing our egos. Feeding our egos out of proportion to reach a state where the ego is present in all our endeavors due to lack of under-processing it. The values and virtues we saw in the previous chapter get snowed under.

6. *Over-production*: The waste caused by an accumulation of ego. We are in a perpetual state of ego over-production. Our energy and effort are directed to the negative/unconstructive thoughts and feelings, into the Planned Obsolescence tactics, which leads to the ill capitalist system as we know it today and which can lead in yourself to a negative and egoistic outlook on life. What do you put energy into, what do you feed? Do you weed, sow and reap a nutritious crop or do you sow ego seeds? What do you expect to reap then?

7. *Defects and rework:* This waste is created by lack of inner work. The lack of inner work enables the flourishing of immoral and unethical practices, of a loser and winner mentality. The result is it requires correcting (external) mistakes made, explaining, accounting for, taking responsibility for and saying you are sorry (either meant or not). What should be done instead is correcting your inner errors and eliminating definitively the root cause of the problem.

Muri, overburden, is not only applicable to overburdening others, for instance your employees, but also yourself. How much pressure do you put on yourself, what is your self-image and what do you do to keep up that self-image? Is the self-image really something you want or is it to live up to what others expect of you? Are you a workaholic? Are you only happy and satisfied when you work? Are you stressed? Have you asked yourself why?

Overburdening yourself and others leads to stress, which leads to unproductiveness and a lower performance and creativity than a company should want. In the previous chapter we looked at organizational trauma and neurotic organizations. There is an interesting experiment in New Zealand with a four-day workweek. Perpetual Guardian introduced a four-day workweek but paid their employees for five days. The University of Auckland and the Auckland University of Technology surveyed the eight-week trial period and observed staff stress levels went down from 45% to 38%, while the work-life balance improved from 54% to 78%. The press statements of the company's founder Andrew Barnes speak for themselves: "Our leadership team reported that there was broadly no change in company outputs pre and during the trial. They perceived no reduction in job performance and the survey data showed a marginal increase across most teams." He also says: "What we've seen is a massive increase in engagement and staff satisfaction about the work they do, a massive increase in staff intention to continue to work with the company and we've seen no drop in productivity … We're paying for productivity. We're making a clear distinction here between the amount of hours you spend in the office and what we get out of that."

As a matter of fact, research (Melbourne Institute Working Paper) in Australia suggests that working more than 25 hours when you are over 40 could affect your cognitive performance. Working less than 25 as well so there is a balance to be found for the amount of working hours to be crammed into a day or week. One of the researchers, Colin McKenzie from Keio University in Japan says: "In all three cases it was found around 25–30 hours of work per week will maximize your cognitive skills … For cognitive functioning, working far too much is worse than not working at all." Stress is known to have a very detrimental effect on our cognitive abilities; it kills brain neurons. Aren't (ICT) companies aiming to do things smarter, work smarter?

And Mura, unevenness? How consistent and stable are you? This waste is when you often have ups and downs and mood swings. Do you have an inner core, an inner stability which isn't shaken or cracked by inner saboteurs or by being victim of inner demons? To what degree do these demons influence your business decision making and dealings out there?

When we learn to auto observe and become aware of our inner workings—thoughts and feelings—and routines, we will be able to understand why and how we interact and communicate with others, which transactions are taking place and who is communicating: our Parent, Adult or Child? To communicate constructively and maturely with our customers, suppliers, partners, stakeholders and employees we must agree on the terms of communication and the words used.

Harris in *I'm OK—You're OK* writes: "Problem solvers, whether international or hometown, talk incessantly about the 'need for dialogue' without ever considering the need to define the terms. In Transactional Analysis we have developed a system unique in (1) its definition of terms and (2) its reduction of behavior to a basic unit of observation. Dialogue, if it is to get us anywhere, must be based on agreement of what to examine and an agreement on the words to describe what we observe. Otherwise we simply stumble over words. A person who had known Sirhan Sirhan reported: 'He was a fanatic about his country, about political things—but no, he was not unstable'. Words like 'fanatic' and 'unstable' are useless in analyzing or predicting behavior. Many of our dialogues are useless for the same reason. Much is said, but nothing is understood." We say much, we have so many inner ego voices, we don't understand ourselves anymore, least of all others. We have replaced Hamlet's "to be or not to be", for "to win or not to win." To win has become more important than to be, and we must win because otherwise we lose … that has become the raison d'être of modern man.

WHAT TO DO WITH ALL THESE FRAMEWORKS AND MODELS

I have discussed various frameworks, methodologies and best practices in the previous chapters and have commented on how we use them, their benefits and also, in my opinion, their omissions. The fact that they are useful to oversee, get a grip on and be in control of our service delivery and support as service providers is clear. The same goes for customers and suppliers. They all have their added value, *when* they are implemented and used properly, *when* we adhere to them, *when* we continue using our common sense and *when* we truly understand why we want to use them and what we are trying to achieve.

They are not magical solutions to our woes, but they do help us streamline the work, information and communication flows within our own company as well as help the interactions with our customers and suppliers and all other stakeholders. However, the Planned Obsolescence system we have created pushes the methodologies, best practices, models etc. into the same focus on speed, due to the shortening of the replacement cycle, *within* the methodology itself, e.g. processes which need to be continuously sped up and be ever more efficient and agile, usually at the cost of attention to quality. Additionally the speed factor implies "replacing" or adding new frameworks or best practices. Not only does Planned Obsolescence apply to the products or services which are churned out faster and faster, but it is directed to the methodologies etc. as well. They are falling into the same ICT fast food trap which is a shame, because the benefits of the frameworks, methodologies and best practices, if applied well and thoroughly, are numerous.

The question we must ask ourselves is if the frameworks etc. address our organizational issues adequately. This means, first of all, we have to understand what those issues are and what drives us in our business dealings. Since we have an economic system which, as I have recounted in the previous chapters, is ill and unbalanced, it can be worthwhile to have a closer look at the models and approaches we use every day and consider useful and constructive to manage our companies.

Are our assumptions regarding the completeness and holistic-ness correct or are we using an approach which is actually damaging us or even fomenting the Planned Obsolescence reality we have created? The balanced Scorecard by Kaplan and Norton (1996) is a strategic planning and management system which addresses all the relevant aspects to manage an organization successfully, or differently put, looks at an organization from different perspectives so that all elements are considered which influence the performance of the organization. These perspectives are:

- *Financial*: focus on the financial condition and performance
- *Customer*: focus on customer satisfaction and customer value
- *Internal processes*: focus on the workflows to obtain the desired results
- *Organizational capacity (originally called Learning and Growth)*: focus on development and growth in skills and capacity of employees to face the future challenges

The ingrained assumption is that the values a company strives for are ethically sound, but we have seen that we cannot count on that fact at all anymore, especially in the ICT sector. We have seen that moral decision making and ethical business behavior cannot stay in the realm of assumptions and/or expectations. The basic, core trust in organizations, profit and non-profit, needed to be able to do business, live in a constructive democratic (business) world and safeguard that world, have been eroded by lack of attention to it and by ego driven "values."

As recent as December 2018 we read about Facebook offering users' data to other companies, such as Amazon and Microsoft. Internal documents obtained by the New York Times show the arrangement to share its users' data with more than 150 companies, and in such a way Facebook's usual privacy rules were avoided. The Cambridge Analytica stench is still with us. Netflix and Spotify had the "ability to read Facebook users' private messages," the report said. It is not only unethical to offer the data, it is also unethical to accept the offered information of users who have not given permission to share their personal details.

It is mentioned the trust in Facebook, and in the majority of other ICT companies for that matter, must be regained. Excuse me? You cannot regain trust with empty promises it will not happen again and by being, supposedly, more in control, with extra attention to security and privacy, etc. Those are actions *out there*. While the immorality *in here* is not addressed and eliminated, nothing will change *out there* and all it is, is window dressing. Facebook, Apple, Google and all those companies who have taken advantage of the possibility to read people's *private* messages, are continuously lying through their teeth, even in a congressional hearing's setting. No, there is something profoundly rotten in the state of Silicon Valley.

So if we cannot trust and adopt the basic stance that companies are ethical in their dealings, we will have to focus specifically on the ethics, to avoid avoiding it. The balanced scorecard could do with a fifth perspective, the ethical one. This idea is not new. When I reached this conclusion myself and investigated if anyone else had ever come up with this idea, I saw that indeed, Paul Arveson, co-founder of the Balanced Scorecard Institute, published an article on the institute's site in 2002 proposing either adding the ethical perspective to the original dimension of Learning and Growth or adding it as a fifth perspective. Both could apply of course but my preference goes to adding it as a separate perspective so that you have to pay the necessary attention to it.

Paul Arveson writes: "Sound business ethics must be *practiced* in order to rebuild trust in a company, and in our entire economic system. Underlying all of the other features of a healthy organization, there must be an abundance of good will, transparency and ethical behavior. Because of the pervasive importance of customer and investor trust, I suggest that *ethical business behavior* should be included in the 'learning and growth' perspective of the balanced scorecard, or that *an ethical business culture* should be added as a fifth perspective where appropriate." He goes a step further because recognizing the need to be able to measure ethical practices, he presents metrics which can be used. He introduces them the following way:

> But how can you *measure* ethical performance? Balanced scorecard designers, of course, routinely encounter aspects of performance that are qualitative and hard to measure. Perhaps this is the hardest—but it is not impossible. Based on the principles that 'he who is faithful in the least will be faithful also in much' and 'a tree is known by its fruit,' here are some possible metrics to consider (metrics with asterisks (*) are also relevant in public-sector organizations).

I have taken the liberty to expand on the metrics and added my contributions in italic.

Metric	Rationale
Level of business ethics training*	Modern business is complex; we must not assume that the rules of ethical behavior are known without training and evaluation of employees. This could also include training on the company's own business principles. *Do leaders and managers on strategic level participate as well?* *Training on the economic model the company employs and its ethical implications.*
Morale of employees*	If a company doesn't treat its own employees fairly, how fair can it be to outsiders?
Treatment of employees	*What language is used when addressing employees and when addressing difficult issues?* *How do they treat employees in other countries? The different treatment of employees in other countries and the conditions they work in can be an indicator of the values these companies live by.*
*Development and training**	*How much time does the employee receive to study, participate in events and/or attend a training? Who pays?*
Openness, transparency*	Do executives hide behind spin and obfuscation? Is there a lot of secrecy? *Are employees involved and/or communicated with about the company's direction and policies?*
Candor*	Do leaders report bad news as well as good news? Are they self-critical? Do they take responsibility? *Can employees be critical and/or disagree or will there be repercussions?*
Turnover rate*	If high, may indicate employee dissatisfaction. *If high, it may indicate high stress levels. Why do they feel stress, what kind is it and who/what creates it? Can employees grow within the organization? Are they treated with respect, listened to, asked why they do things in a certain manner?*
Union relations*	If constantly strained, may indicate perceptions of distrust by employees. *Are employees pressured not to be members of unions and if so, what does that pressure consist of?*

(Continued)

Metric	Rationale
Hotline*	Do employees have access to an anonymous communication channel to managers or inspectors?
Nepotism*	It may be more likely for family members to share dishonest practices, to exclude more-qualified managers, or to be distracted by infighting.
Old-Boys network	*Are the same people hopping from company to company, occupying the same type of positions? What is the price?* *Is corporate inbreeding taking place?*
Track record	*What is the track record of leaders? (success and failure, average time at a company, leadership style, organizational culture created, risk taking, etc.)*
Contracts	*Is there a balance between responsibility and accountability and the salary received? Is there a bonus structure and if so, what are the incentives and how high are the bonuses? What kind of behavior can this bonus structure encourage?*
Leadership style	*The leadership style, e.g. a very autocratic one, can be an indicator of not enough transparency and/or of a neurotic leader.*
Community involvement*	Do the managers care about their neighbors? *Do they care about the societies and countries they operate in? Do they respect the local customs?*
Criminal records*	Public records may be available for some executives.
Driving records*	Bad driving may be a symptom of other problems.
Extravagance*	Managers' use of corporate resources, opulence of buildings, homes, etc. may be excessive. *Do they travel in 1st or 2nd class?*
Environmental awareness*	*Do they leave all the lights on? Do they recycle? Do they pollute?* *Do they respect the environment, also when they do business in other countries?* *Do they dump their waste, and where?* *How much waste do they create?*
Employee policies*	Are employee policies in line with industry, or excessively stringent? *Are there different rules for managers/ leaders and for the rest of the employees?* *Is there a clear job performance/assessment interview system, is it transparent and can employees protest if they don't agree? Is there an independent entity where they can address these issues?*

(Continued)

Metric	Rationale
Resignations*	Executive resignations, other than for age, may indicate conflicts.
	A high percentage of resignations across the company, on all levels can indicate internal dissatisfaction and/or conflict.
Employee diversity*	Is it representative of the general population?
Whistleblowers*	If any, what are they saying? How are they treated?
	Is it indicative there is a culture of non-acceptance of issues being raised?
Inspectors, regulators*	US govt. agencies—see Inspector General reports. Stock investors should check the *EDGAR* database. For occupational safety, check for *OSHA* violations. For foods and drugs, check the *FDA*. For consumer products, check *CPSC*. For vehicles, check *NHTSA*.
Transparency*	Financial and related company data should be reported frequently and openly on websites.
Charitable giving; foundations	Altruistic behavior is difficult for crooks.
	Are charities being used for other purposes than charity?
Work hours	Long hours mean stressed employees.
	How many extra hours do employees work and how many are remunerated and not remunerated?
	How often are employees requested/pressured to work extra?
	Are employees pressured to participate in activities outside work hours? Does it have repercussions when they don't attend?
Lobbying expenses	Excessive, multi-party lobbying efforts were an Enron trademark.
Lobbying practices	*Are they legal? Should they be forbidden?*
	The amount of effort, apart from the expenses, can raise questions on the interests involved.
	The strong involvement of companies with lobbying can be an indicator of the degree to which they can be influenced. At what price?
Legal expenses	Too many lawsuits and lawyers on the payroll may indicate a defensive or aggressive culture.
Insider trading	New rules require prompt reporting within days.
Taxes paid	No taxes? Maybe the company is being too clever.
Cash flow	Better indicator of health than stock price.
Dividends	Company cannot cheat with payouts of dividends.

(Continued)

Metric	Rationale
401(K) plans	May employees invest other than in company stock?
Stock options	Are they expensed?
Bond ratings	Indicates analysts' estimates of company's ability to pay its debts.
Social responsibility	Is company stock included in a socially responsible mutual fund? (See *lists*)
Financial institutions used	*Are the financial institutions such as banks (morally) sound?*
	Which accounting firms are used by the companies? What is their track record?

How balanced is the balanced scorecard if we don't pay attention to who we are and how we act? To be (ethical) or not to be, that is the question.

In the same vein as the metrics of ethical performance mentioned above, I would like to highlight the Quality Impact monitor Dr. Klamer introduces in his book *Doing the Right Thing—A value—based economy*. To use his own words: "The quality impact monitor is designed to monitor the realization of values or qualities. It provides leaders of organizations with clear indications of what to do, of what to change in their strategies, and it provides funders and supervisors a clear perspective on the effectiveness of the organization in realizing its goals." The people involved in the development of the Quality Impact monitor seek to contribute to achieving another economics for another economy. As Klamer puts it: "I expect and hope that we will leave the dominance of instrumentalist thinking behind us, and it becomes normal to think of substantive qualities first before we consider quantities."

Another model which could add the ethical dimension is CMMI (Capability Maturity Model Integration) developed at Carnegie Mellon University. Originally applied to software development and focused on the capability levels of processes and their improvement, the model, administered by the CMMI Institute, a subsidiary of ISACA, has developed to include CMMI covering the range of People, Process and Technology such as CMMI for Services, Supplier Management, People, Cyber Maturity and Data Management Maturity. The capability and maturity levels identified are 5, ranging from the least to the most capable or mature level: Initial, Managed, Defined, Managed, and Optimizing. A CMMI for Ethics would put the topic on the map and to the forefront of business and would permit assessments and/or audits. Who dares to be assessed or audited on ethical ICT business dealings and data sharing?

In the previous chapters COBIT 5 was mentioned and that one of its 7 enablers is Culture, Ethics and Behavior. The combined enablers (Principles, Policies and Frameworks, Processes, Organizational Structures, Information, Services, Infrastructure & Applications, People, Skills and Competences and the one I already mentioned) influence ICT governance and management. ISACA has clearly identified the factors important for governance and management; now we urgently need the official guide on this topic as well as on the People, Skills and Competencies since they are closely related and long overdue.

Included in practically all frameworks, models and methodologies is the concept of continuous improvement. The necessity for continuous improvement in processes, people and technology related issues is an accepted must and when incorporated in the numerous old and new best practices we will encounter Dr. W. Edwards Deming with the Deming Cycle, Circle or Deming Wheel. It is also known as the PDCA cycle: Plan-Do-Check-Act. This is not correct and not how Deming presented nor intended it. Since the PDCA has led to practices and a focus I also personally think is not the way to go, I will expound on the matter.

Dr. Deming himself referred to the PDSA cycle: Plan, Do, Study, Act. He also called it the Shewhart cycle, in reference to his mentor, Walter Shewhart, from Bell Laboratories in New York. Dr. Shewhart was a physician and his ideas on industrial quality, science and statistical inference inspired Deming to adopt some of his methodological approaches into what he named the Shewhart cycle. The cycle has been revised and enhanced over time, including by Deming himself. In the 1980s he reintroduced the PDSA cycle, with emphasis on the S of Study warning the Check of the PDCA cycle is inaccurate because the word Check means: "to hold back." In 1993 he renamed the Shewhart Cycle the Shewhart Cycle for Learning and Improvement—improvement of a product or process. Deming made a very clear distinction between the PDCA and the PDSA cycle. Figure 4.1 illustrates the Shewhart cycle with the step Study.

The Deming Institute offers a link to an illuminating article by Ron Moen and Cliff Norman on the subject, named *Circling Back—Clearing up myths about the Deming cycle and seeing how it keeps evolving*. Asked about the differences between the cycles Deming says: "They bear no relation to each other," Deming said. "The Deming circle (PDCA) is a quality control program. It is a plan for management. Four steps: Design it,

FIGURE 4.1
The Shewhart cycle (PDSA). The Deming PDSA cycle is different from the PDCA cycle because it includes Study instead of Check. Study implies taking the time, making the effort and being curious to understand if the results of your intended improvement correspond with your hopes and expectations and if not, what went wrong.

make it, sell it, then test it in service. Repeat the four steps, over and over, redesign it, make it, etc. Maybe you could say that the Deming circle is for management, and the QC (Quality Control) circle is for a group of people that work on faults encountered at the local level." To avoid any misunderstanding on Deming's opinion on the matter I cite again from the article: "On Nov. 17, 1990, Deming wrote a letter to Ronald D. Moen to comment on the manuscript for *Improving Quality Through Planned Experimentation,* coauthored by Moen, Thomas R. Nolan and Lloyd P. Provost. "Be sure to call it PDSA, not the corruption PDCA," Deming wrote in the letter. In response to a letter he received in 1991, Deming commented about a chart labeled plan-do-check-act. "What you propose is not the Deming cycle," he wrote in the letter. "I don't know the source of the cycle that you propose. How the PDCA ever came into existence I know not.""

The Deming cycle, PDCA, seemed to have come into existence by adaptation's made by the Japanese, when Deming presented the Deming wheel (being the Shewhart cycle) to them in 1950. Apparently it was recast as the Deming PDCA cycle. "According to Masaaki Imai, Japanese executives recast the Deming wheel presented in the 1950 JUSE seminars into the PDCA cycle … Imai did not provide details about which executives reworked the wheel or how they translated the Deming wheel into the PDCA cycle. No one has ever claimed ownership of this revision or disputed Imai's assertion."

So what did Deming mean with the PDSA cycle? Plan refers to planning of change or of a test (for improvement or innovation), Do is carrying out the change or the test. The latter on a small scale to see what the effects are. Study is studying, examining the results of your improvement. Do the results correspond with your hopes and expectations (his words) and if not, what went wrong? Act is adopting or abandoning the change, or going through the cycle again, under different environmental conditions, to see if you get the same results, or not (The similarities with the Six Sigma DMAIC cycle is clear).

What I would like to highlight and compare is the S, Study in regards with the C, Check of the PDCA cycle. As I stated before the PDCA cycle, named Deming cycle, is presented and used in relation to multiple other frameworks and in the related courses taught worldwide. Check is presented and explained as checking to see if what you did (Do), went according to the plan (Plan). In practice this has become, literally, a check according to a checklist to see if a company, a service provider for example, complies with the KPIs. Responding to customer requirements and achieving customer satisfaction has evolved into being able to check off a catalogue of KPIs. There is no studying or examining going on to truly understand the matter, but as long as you smartly respect the long list of KPIs you have to comply with, you seem to be on the safe side. No mistake, respecting KPIs is necessary, but it seems customer satisfaction and service delivery and support have become cleverly being able to tick off a litany of KPIs. And when there is an issue of non-compliance with KPIs, it seems to be more about understanding and interpreting complex calculations on how you got the result you have and how to creatively tweak numbers, than of delving into, studying and examining what went wrong and why, as Deming stated and intended. Do the results correspond with your, and the customer's hopes and expectations?

It is another example of an over emphasis or worse, sole emphasis, in my opinion, on the quantification of customer satisfaction and responding to customer expectations and needs encouraged by the use of the word Check, and its tempting invitation to a dualistic interpretation: comply or not comply with KPIs. Apart from avoiding a rewriting of history and doing injustice to the ideas of Shewhart and Deming, the limited and incorrect application of their contributions and our interpretation of them enables practices which are not doing us any favors, as we have seen. Our KPI obsession and thinking that as long as they are complied with we, the customer, get what we want, we, the service provider are complying with and respecting the contract and we, the suppliers, idem ditto. If that is so, why is there so much dissatisfaction among the three parties? What I propose is to go back to the Shewhart and Deming basics and study with a discerning mind and a true desire to improve in act(ion).

Top executives and managers need more psychological insight. It is not enough to just have the skills to interpret Excel sheets, but the capability to understand people is necessary. To quote Deming: "It would be better if everyone worked together as a system, with the aim for everybody to win." And to finalize: "We must preserve the power of intrinsic motivation, dignity, cooperation, curiosity, joy in learning, that people are born with."

RESPONSIBILITY AND ACCOUNTABILITY ... OH DEAR

Whether we are a consumer, a producer, an employee, a manager or an executive on C-level we are individuals who make choices every single day within the personal and social context about our attitude and behavior towards ourselves and towards others. We choose what we stand for in (business) life, the values we consider important and if we want to act ethically. We are responsible and accountable for our thoughts, feelings and actions. Additionally, we are responsible and accountable for what we project into the world, what we do onto others, how we interact and what we create.

As a group of people, either in an organizational context, family context, national and global context we carry collective responsibility and accountability as well. Every single day, as the collective, from small to big, we make choices about our attitude and behavior. Some take up the responsibility and act taking the common interests of the bigger whole into consideration; many fade into an unanimous role within the group; hidden in numbers and therefore "free" to express their inner disequilibrium into the outside world and create another type of reality as a result.

When we look at the state of affairs in business, what drives us, what we have projected and are still projecting into and onto the (business) world, when we look at the kind of (economic) reality we have created we can only conclude that we are not taking responsibility for our collective thoughts and actions.

The (ab)use of ICT and big tech are the ultimate expression of the ill and misbalanced reality we have created. Not ill for existing, but for the profound abuse of trust, decency and integrity. With them we have passed to the other side; the side where defrauding your "customers" by harvesting their data, selling it, sharing it with anyone, lying through your teeth about it, and making loads of money in the process is the norm. Where the common interest is not even on their list of priorities, where distracting people with overpriced gadgets is their desire; the more distraction, the less the masses think, discern and make conscious decisions, the easier they are to influence and manipulate. And we all go along with it, enchanted by the magical tune. Collectively, we have completely lost the plot.

As long as we do not feel and take responsibility, as long as people, individually and collectively, and organizations are not held accountable for the unhealthy Planned Obsolescence (ICT) business dealings, nothing will change for the better and our reality will deteriorate with increasing speed. The manner in which we use social media is a symptom of our inner state; we have a medium for instant reaction, where we look for validation and where we can immerse ourselves within the masses, the new tribe we wish to belong to.

Social media permits us to fling our mental and emotional diarrhea into the ether. Putting it all out there is actually putting the responsibility outside yourself for your thinking and feeling; validation for existing and being is craved from the other. Social media fosters reactiveness and is a wonderful outlet for all people who prefer not to think about things too much; not too much reflection, not too much digestion, please. The inner indigestion is due to lack of feeding ourselves with healthy and nutritious food and chewing on it; instead we gulp down in an instant. It seems a lot of people consider life as a fast food opera.

As for responsibility and accountability: people who uninhibitedly film and record other people without their consent and publish it on social media for the masses to consume, are just as guilty of violating privacy and personal space they accuse the big tech companies of doing. If you don't condone companies abusing your privacy and personal information, don't do it yourself.

Governance in these times, and especially since the financial excesses and crises, is high on the agenda. It is a word readily used but is it as readily acted upon? Governance is the responsibility of the board of directors, executives and non-executives. Are they taking it? Have things changed since the 2002 Sarbanes-Oxley act? SOX or Sarbox is also known, in the Senate, as the "Public Company Accounting Reform and Investor Protection Act" and in the House as "Corporate and Auditing Accountability, Responsibility, and Transparency Act." Are (ICT) corporations being held accountable, responsible and are they transparent? It is in our faces they are not. So what is being done about it, apart from saying how terrible it is? Perhaps a Sarbanes-Oxley for ICT and big tech is needed.

Governments and states who take their responsibility and who feel accountable for making decisions and acting for the common good and general interest are more necessary than ever, but generally very wanting. They seem to suffer from an identity crisis and not know what they are for. They should ask themselves what they stand for, which values they consider important and whom they serve. How do they serve the people who have given them their trust to govern decently, transparently and responsibly? Do they remember that they are *serving*? Is the trust citizens put in them deserved or is it misplaced? Have they jumped on the bandwagon of corporations and the Planned Obsolescence look on life and are they capable of seeing and perceiving their role as more than in duality terms of consumers and producers? Are the economic quantifiable values the *only* values they see or care about? What and whom are they facilitating and what kind of behavior and practices are they enabling, and even participating actively in themselves? What is their approach to life?

Many questions asked but hardly any time and stillness to contemplate these serious matters. ICT companies have made visual and auditory noise their trademark; there should never be a quiet moment or any silence. These Masters of Mass Distraction get a warm welcome from individuals, groups, companies and nations to help keep everyone away from turning attention inward, from asking the important and difficult questions (about values) and from merely being. The intimacy of yourself, with you and your thoughts and feelings is aggressively targeted, because that is where the real and ultimate power lies: within.

Graham Turner in the book *The Power of Silence* (2012) writes about the meaning and importance of silence for people around the world. He quotes a Hindu friend who says: "After all, it's in silence that we reflect on the truths we have come across in life. Everything is born in silence—all thoughts, all wisdom, all perspective. Without it, you'll never see things as they really are, you'll always be ruled by your reactions—and, as those reactions prey on your mind and increase in intensity, it'll ruin your peace."

Silence is practiced deliberately by people who meditate. Meditation, or mindfulness as some like to call it in the West, is usually done sitting in an upright position. Apart from having an effect on your body it has an effect on your mind.

> First, you're looking at yourself and, in the beginning, you are disturbed by what you see. Then you get tired of being disturbed by what you see, meaning that you get tired of your own ego, your own baggage—and what is more boring than your own baggage?

In companies we have a smoking room to cater to an addiction. Why not a silence room, a place for non-distraction:no phones, no bleeps, no rings, no chatter. No pictures taken, no video watched, no social media consumed. Just silence, peace and harmony. It could help us get in touch with ourselves, our values and listen to our inner voice. Surprise, we could even begin to understand ourselves and others better. This might sound strange for some but scheduled silence time exists and is fully accepted in some parts of the world and functions successfully.

For example, in 2007 in India, The Mata Amritanandamayi Math (MAM is an international charitable organization aimed at the spiritual and material upliftment of humankind) undertook a massive project of teaching the 20 minutes modern day IAM Technique® (Integrated Amrita Meditation Technique®) to India's 2.5 million paramilitary personnel. This technique has also been taught in the software company Infosys, BSNL (Bharat Sanchar Nigam Limited, a giant public sector undertaking Indian Telephone Industries) and IIM (Indian Institute of Management, the premier management institute of the country).

This IAM Technique® is taught because the institutions and companies understand its benefits and are open and willing to offer the quiet time to turn inward for their employees. The fact it is taught free of charge says it all. To quote Amma, the founder of MAM and creator of this meditation technique: "The remote control of our mind should rest firmly in the palm of our hand."

On their website (https://www.amritapuri.org/activity/cultural/iam) the benefits of the technique are explained: "IAM Meditation Technique is a daily mental maintenance system ... Through focusing on objects, sounds and sensations during meditation, our power of concentration increases. Observing our mental and vital functions, we gain awareness. Relaxing the mind removes stress. Expanding our concept of our self similarly expands our thinking in general, making us more creative." Why not help ourselves and do some much needed maintenance and become healthier in thoughts, feelings and actions?

If there is light in the soul,
There will be beauty in the person.
If there is beauty in the person,
There will be harmony in the house.
If there is harmony in the house,
There will be order in the nation.
If there is order in the nation,
There will be peace in the world.

Chinese proverb

5

Conclusion

We have looked at the world of service providers, customers and suppliers and how they interact with each other. We have seen what the basis is of our economic business life, where it came from and what made it so. We have seen the consequences in organizations and on a larger scale, on the market and on the economy globally. What we are doing—or better still what we are NOT doing—is having severe consequences and impact on the health of organizations, societies, countries and on the planet.

We try to patch things up and find solutions with better workflows, better frameworks and methodologies, better agreements, better oversight, etc. But what we continue avoiding and not addressing is ourselves, as creators of the reality and the world we have crystallized into being on this planet. If we look at where we stand: what have we created? Are we proud of it? Which values rule our world? What we have not done for centuries is work on ourselves. We have not developed internally, we have not confronted ourselves. We have let our shadow side let rip and let it manifest itself in the (business) interactions we know today. We are responsible and accountable for what we have manifested and what we feed. What do we feed? Positive values or greed, anger, fear, etc.

Have we advanced as professionals, have we progressed as human beings? Are we proud of what we have been doing up till now and if we are not, and we see the truths we uphold are causing damage to others and as a consequence to ourselves, do we have the courage to change? Are we capable of a bit of humility, respect, admitting we have taken the wrong turn and are on a side road leading us over the cliff? Will we continue sticking our heads in the sand and say go away, go away or just look the other way? What are we made of?

The personal and collective projection and extrapolation of our inner world onto and into the world at large has created a reality that is about consumption, taking (and no or little giving) and abuse of trust, privacy, decency and authenticity in our (business) interactions. If planned obsolescence is the name of the game, yes, as a result we will have planned obsolescence of the resources available to us, including the human resource. We have maneuvered ourselves into a self-fulfilling prophecy loop of unawareness, unconsciousness and (self-)destruction, speeded up by ICT and big tech.

Do we point our finger at the other and say it is their fault, they started it, etc., or do we have the guts to point the finger at ourselves and have a long, hard look at what we are thinking, feeling and doing? Who are we?

The organizational neurosis, result of our personal neurosis, is being enacted by us in our institutions and organizations. It defines how we interact with others on a small and global scale and how we interact with the planet. We are ill and our illness is visible in our way of doing business, in the so-called values we uphold, in the economic model we sustain, in the way we perceive and treat our neighbor and how we live on and with the living organism which sustains us, our planet. Will we do the work to improve our personal health and that of our family, work and natural environment? The work is from the inside out. Who dares to confront himself and look himself in the eye? The Greek inscription in the forecourt of the temple of Apollo in Delphi, where the oracle is, tells us: Know Thyself.

ICT and technology provide us with many advantages and can benefit us greatly, *if* it is used with phronesis, *if* it is used for the good and interest of all and *if* moral values and ethical business decisions are prevalent. Unfortunately, as long as the human being doesn't weed out the inner waste, fear and ego-driven urges, use will always lead to abuse and poison something that originally was well intended.

The big tech companies' démasqué—we read about it every day in multiple cases—shows ICT has moved from the use to the abuse qualification and ICT, albeit its multiple benefits, can be seen, in the manner we apply it today, as the ultimate crystallization into the outside world, the ultimate expression of a severely misbalanced society and capitalist system. This is what we have created from the inside out.

Leaders, C-suite executives, strategic managers and any other person in a position whose decisions shape and impact a bigger group, be it in a profit or non-profit organization, be it on a regional, national or global level have an extra and major responsibility. Being in a position of responsibility, means exactly that, being responsible: in decisions, in actions, in communication, in treatment of others etc. The higher the position, the more responsibility and accountability you have. Do you see it as such, or do you take the duality inspired feeling and thinking: I am the winner, the others are losers? Do you enjoy the position of power and the amount of money you are making for the sake of it, or do we feel the weight of responsibility, to do the right thing, right, at the right moment?

In the preface I wrote the intention of this book was to slow down a moment and take time for some reflection and contemplation. I invited you to put your feet on your desk, sit back and delve together with me into the depths of the ICT labyrinth and confront all that we encountered with courage along the way. I hope the discoveries you made were worthwhile and will help you in your own endeavors, from the inside out.

For those when reading this book who consider it naïve to think we can change an economic system, the current way of business interactions and of living a value-based life: I think it is naïve to think we can continue on this track. And something else: is this the best mankind can do, having arrived at the twenty-first century? Is this our best creation?

Bibliography

Ashkenas, Ron, Ulrich, Dave, Jick, Todd, Kerr, Steve, *The Bounderyless Organization, Breaking the Chains of Organizational Structure*, Jossey-Bass, A Wiley Imprint, San Francisco, CA, 2002.

Berne, Eric, *A Layman's Guide to Psychiatry and Psychoanalysis*, Ballantine Books, New York, 1947 and 1957.

Berne, Eric, *Beyond Games and Scripts*, Selections from His Major Writings, edited by Claude Steiner and Carmen Kerr, Ballantine Books, New York, 1976.

Berne, Eric, *Games People Play*, Grove Press, New York, 1964.

Berne, Eric, *The Structure and Dynamics of Organizations and Groups*, Ballantine Books, New York, 1963.

Berne, Eric, *Principles of Group Treatment*, Vintage, New York, 1971.

Burnes, *Bernard, Managing Change, A Strategic Approach to Organisational Dynamics*, Pearson Educational Limited, Harlow, UK, 2004.

Carnegie Mellon University, Software Engineering Institute, *The Capability Maturity Model: Guidelines for Improving the Software Process*, Addison Wesley, Reading, MA, 1994.

Crisp, Roger, *Aristotle: Nicomachean Ethics*, Cambridge University Press, Cambridge, MA, 2002.

Daft, Richard L., *Organization Theory & Design*, West Publishing Company, St. Paul, MI, 1995.

Deighton, Paul and Nutt, Howard, *The Capability Maturity Model® for Business Development, Version 2.02*, APMP Center for Business Development Excellence, Phoenix, AZ, 2016.

Deming, W. Edwards, *The New Economics for Industry, Government, and Education*, MIT Press, Boston, MA, 1993.

Deming, W. Edwards, *Out of the Crisis*, MIT Press, Cambridge, MA, 1986.

Duhigg, Charles, *The Power of Habit, Why We Do What We Do in Life and Business*, Random House Trade Paperback edition, New York, 2014.

Elliott, Charles, *Locating the Energy for Change: An Introduction to Appreciative Inquiry*, International Institute for Sustainable Development, Winnipeg, Canada, 1999.

Englisch, Brigitte, *Ordo orbis terrae: Die Weltsicht in den Mappae mundi des frühen und hohen Mittelalters*, De Gruyter Akademie Forschung, Berlin, Germany, 2002.

Floridi, Luciano, *The Cambridge Handbook of Information and Computer Ethics*, Cambridge University Press, Cambridge, 2010.

Foer, Franklin, *World Without Mind, The Existential Threat of Big Tech*, Penguin Press, New York, 2017. Kindle edition.

Foot, Philippa, *Natural Goodness*, Clarendon Press, Gloucestershire, UK, 2013.

Glassner, Barry, *The Culture of Fear, Why Americans are Afraid of the Wrong Things*, Basic Books, New York, 1999. Kindle edition.

Gleeson-White, Jane, *Double Entry, How the Merchants of Venice Created Modern Finance*, W.W. Norton & Company, New York, 2011.

Greenberg, Jerald, Baron, Robert A., *Behavior in Organizations*, Pearson Prentice Hall, Upper Saddle River, NJ, 2008.

Hannah, Barbara, *Jung, His Life and Work*, Michael Joseph, London, UK, 1977.

Harris, Thomas A., *I'm OK-You're OK, A Practical Guide to Transactional Analysis*, Harper & Row, New York, 1967.

Holman, Peggy, Devane, Tom, Cady, Steven and Associates, *The Change Handbook, A Definitive Resource on Today's Best Methods for Engaging Whole Systems*, Berret-Koehler Publishers, San Francisco, CA, 2007.

Jung: *C.G. Jung Speaking: Interviews and Encounters*, edited by William McGuire and R.F.C. Hull, Picador, London, UK, 1980.

Jung, Carl Gustav, *Psychology and Religion*, Bollingen Series, Princeton University Press, Princeton, NJ, 1969.

Jung C.G., *Memoires, Dreams, Reflections*, recorded and edited by Aniela Jaffe, Collins and Routledge & Kegan Paul, London, UK, 1963.

Jung, *The Cambridge Companion to*, edited by Polly Young-Eisendrath and Terence Dawson, Cambridge University Press, New York, 2008.

Kets de Vries, Manfred, *The Leader on the Couch, A Clinical Approach to Changing People and Organizations*, Jossey-Bass, A Wiley Imprint, Chichester, UK, 2006.

Kets de Vries, Manfred F.R., Korotov, Konstantin, Florent-Treacy, Elizabeth and Rook, Caroline, *Coach and Couch, The Psychology of Making Better Leaders*, Palgrave MacMillan, Hampshire, 2016. Kindle edition.

Keuning, D., Eppink, D.J., *Management & Organisatie, theorie en toepassing*, Wolters-Noordhoff, Groningen, the Netherlands, 2004.

Kimman, Eduard, *Verkaveling van de moraal, Inleiding bedrijfsethiek*, Rozenberg Publishers, Amsterdam, the Netherlands, 2006.

Klamer, Arjo, *Doing The Right Thing, A Value Based Economy*, Society of Economics and Culture (SEC), Hilversum, 2016.

Klamer, Arjo, McCloskey, Deirdre and Ziliak, Stephen, *The Economic Conversation*, Palgrave MacMillan, London, UK, 2015.

Kotter, John P., *Leading Change*, Harvard Business School Press, Boston, MA, 1996.

MacIntyre, Alasdair, *After Virtue: A Study in Moral Theory*, University of Notre Dame Press, Notre Dame, IN, 1981

Morozov, Evgeny, *To save Everything, Click Here, The Folly of Technological Solutionism*, Public Affairs, New York, 2013.

Nelson, Richard R. and Winter, Sidney G., *An Evolutionary Theory of Economic Change*, The Belknap Press of Harvard University Press, Cambridge, MA, 1982.

Nussbaum, Martha C. *The Fragility of Goodness: Luck and Ethics in Greek Tragedy and Philosophy*, Cambridge University Press, New York, 1986.

Pacioli, Luca, *Summa de arithmetica, geometria, proportioni et proportionalita*, Paganini, Venice, 1494.

Packard, Vance, *The People Shapers*, Futura Publications, Camberwell, London, UK, 1978.

Packard, Vance, *The Waste Makers*, IG Publishers, New York, 1960. Kindle edition.

Progroff, Ira, *Jung's Psychology and Its Social Meaning*, Anchor Press/Doubleday, Garden City, New York, 1973.

Reif, Linda C., *The Ombudsman, Good Governance and the International Human Rights System*, Martinus Nijhoff Publishers, Leiden, the Netherlands, 2004.

Schein, Edgar H., *Organizational Leadership and Culture* (4th Edition) Jossey-Bass, San Francisco, CA, 2010.

Schumpeter, Joseph A., *Capitalism, Socialism and Democracy*, Harper and Brothers (Collins), New York, 1942.

Smith, Adam, *The Theory of Moral Sentiments, or An Essay towards An Analysis of the Principles by which Men naturally judge concerning the Conduct and Character, first of their Neighbours, and afterwards of themselves, to which is added a Dissertation on the Origin of Languages.* (Sixth ed.). London: A. Strahan; and T. Cadell in the Strand; and T. Creech and J. Bell & Co. at Edinburgh. Retrieved 18 June 2015.

Turner, Graham, *The Power of Silence, The Riches that Lie Within*, Bloomsbury, London, UK, 2012.

Vivian, Pat and Hormann, Shana, *Organizational Trauma and Healing*, CreateSpace, North Charleston, SC, 2013. Kindle edition.

ARTICLES

Arveson, Paul, *The Ethics Perspective*, published on the Balanced Scorecard Institute's site, 2002.

Axelos, *IT Service management Benchmarking Report 2017, Aligning ITSM and Business Strategy.*

Bechtel, William and Richardson, Robert C., *Vitalism*. In E. Craig (Ed.), Routledge Encyclopedia of Philosophy. Routledge. London, UK. 1998.

Blanc, Louis, *Revue du progres*: L'Organisation du travail. 1839

Bustamante Kuschel, P.G., *Rationality and Phronesis in Economics: A Rhetorical Moment.* Dissertation. Erasmus University Rotterdam, the Netherlands, 2012

Deloitte Insights, *Manifesting legacy: Looking beyond the digital era. 2018 global CIO survey.*

Forbes, The Forbes Insights Survey, *Delivering Value to today's digital enterprise*, 2017.

Gartner, *The 2017 CIO Survey.*

Gartner, *The 2018 CIO Survey.*

Gartner, *The Gartner 2017 CEO Survey: CIOs Must Scale Up Digital Business.*

Gartner, *The Gartner 2018 CEO and Senior Business Executive Survey:CIOs Should Guide Business Leaders Toward Deep-Discipline Digital Business.*

Genesys Global Survey (2009), *The Cost of Poor Customer Service, The Economic Impact of the Customer Experience and Engagement in 16 Key Economies.*

GEP. Insight IT, *Happiness, The Technology Connection between Happiness and Productivity*, 2018.

Help Scout, *Customer Service, 75 Facts, Quotes & Statistics, How Your Business Can Deliver With the Best of the Best*, 2012.

Higgs, Derek, *Review of the role and effectiveness of non-executive directors. Consultation Paper*, 2002.

Institute of Chartered Secretaries and Administrators, *Guidance note: Liability of non-executive directors: Care, skill and diligence*, 2013.

Institute of Directors, *What is the role of the Non-Executive Director?* Factsheet, 2018.

Kajitani, Shinya, McKenzie, Colin and Kei Sakata, Melbourne Institute Working Paper Series, *Working Paper No. 7/16, Use It Too Much and Lose It? The Effect of Working Hours on Cognitive Ability*, The Melbourne University, Australia, 2016.

Kaplan, R.S. and Norton, D.P., *The Balanced Scorecard: Measures that Drive Performance*, Harvard Business Review Press, Boston, MA, 1992.

Kaplan, R.S. and Norton, D.P., *Putting the Balanced Scorecard to Work*, Harvard Business Review Press, Boston, MA, 1993.

Kaplan, R.S. and Norton, D.P., *The Balanced Scorecard: Translating Strategy into Action*, Harvard Business Review Press, Boston, MA, 1996.

Kaplan, R.S. and Norton, D.P., *The Strategy-Focused Organization*, Harvard Business Review Press, Boston, MA, 2000.

London, Bernard, *Ending the Depression Through Planned Obsolescence*, New York, 1932.

Loo van de, Erik, contributed to the book by *Manfred F.R. Kets de Vries. Coach and Couch: The Psychology of Making Better Leaders* (2nd edition, 2016) with an article called *The art of Listening*.

Moen, Ronald D. and Norman, Clifford L., *Circling Back—Clearing up myths about the Deming cycle and seeing how it keeps evolving.* 2010: www.qualityprogress.com.

NEDonBoard, *What to Expect of the NED Role*, 2017.

Nesse, Randolph, in the book *What Will Change Everything,* edited by John Brockman, 2009, contributed the article *Recognizing That The Body Is Not A Machine*, https://www.edge.org/response-detail/11361.

The Committee on the Financial Aspects of Corporate Governance, (known as the Cadbury Committee), *The Financial Aspects of Corporate Governance (The 1992 Cadbury Report)*, 1992.

The University of Auckland and the Auckland University of Technology, *Perpetual Guardian's 4-day workweek trial: Qualitative research analysis*, 2018.

V3, *Top 10 cloud computing risks and concerns*, 2014. https://www.v3.co.uk/v3-uk/news/2343547/top-10-cloud-computing-risks-and-concerns/page/10.

WEBSITES

Eric Berne: http://www.ericberne.com.

IAM – Integrated Amrita Meditation Technique®: https://www.amritapuri.org/activity/cultural/iam.

International Transactional Analysis Association: https://www.itaaworld.org.

The Mata Amritanandamayi Math (MAM): https://www.amritapuri.org.

Urgenda: https://www.urgenda.nl.

METHODOLOGIES, FRAMEWORKS, BEST PRACTICES ETC.

Agile: https://www.agilealliance.org, http: //agilepatterns.org.

CISA: http://www.isaca.org/Certification/CISA-Certified-Information-Systems-Auditor/Pages/default.aspx

CISM: http://www.isaca.org/Certification/CISM-Certified-Information-Security-Manager/Pages/default.aspx

CMMI: https://cmmiinstitute.com/. Includes information on Supply chain (CMMI-ACQ), product and service development (CMMI-DEV), managing and delivering services (CMMI-SVC) and People CMM. CMM is also the basis for a Capability Maturity Model for Business Development.

COBIT 5 (Control Objectives for Information and Related Technology): http://www.isaca.org/COBIT/Pages/COBIT-5.aspx.

DevOps: https://www.devopsagileskills.org,https://devopsinstitute.com.

eTom (Enhanced Telecom Operations Map. In 2013 changed to mean: Business Process Framework):

GEIT (Governance of Enterprise IT): https://www.isaca.org/Knowledge-Center/Research/ResearchDeliverables/Pages/getting-started-with-governance-of-enterprise-it.aspx.

ITIL (Information technology Infrastructure Library): https://www.axelos.com/best-practice-solutions/itil.

Lean IT: https://www.leanitassociation.com/.

MOF (Microsoft Operations Framework): https://docs.microsoft.com/en-us/previous-versions/tn-archive/cc936627(v=technet.10), https://docs.microsoft.com/en-us/biztalk/core/high-availability-and-the-microsoft-operations-framework.

MoP (Management of Portfolios): https://www.axelos.com/best-practice-solutions/mop.

M_O_R (Management of Risk): https://www.axelos.com/best-practice-solutions/mor.

MSP (Managing Successful Programmes): https://www.axelos.com/best-practice-solutions/msp/what-is-msp.

NIST cybersecurity: https://www.nist.gov/cyberframework.

PMBOK (Project Management Body Of Knowledge): https://www.pmi.org/pmbok-guide-standards.

PMP(Project Management Professional): https://www.pmi.org/certifications/types/project-management-pmp.

PRINCE2 (Projects IN Controlled Environments): https://www.axelos.com/best-practice-solutions/prince2.

Resilia: https://www.axelos.com/resilia.

RUP (Rational Unified Process): https://web.archive.org/web/20040402113344/http://www-306.ibm.com/software/awdtools/rup/.

Scrum: https://www.scrum.org.

VeriSM™: https://verism.global/.

XP: http://www.extremeprogramming.org/

Index

Note: Page numbers in italic refer to figures respectively.